GLASGOW ON A PLATE

First published 1999
by Black & White Publishing Ltd, Edinburgh
A B&W Publishing imprint
ISBN 1 902927 00 1
Introduction © Ferrier Richardson 1999
Text & Recipes © The Contributors 1999
Photographs © Alan Donaldson 1999

British Library Cataloguing in Publication Data:
A catalogue record for this book is available
from the British Library.

Design: WINFORTUNE & ASSOCIATES

Alan Donaldson can be contacted on 0141 563 9316

Printed in Spain by Bookprint

ⓖ

GLASGOW ON A PLATE

EDITED BY
FERRIER RICHARDSON

PHOTOGRAPHS BY ALAN DONALDSON

CONTENTS

ACKNOWLEDGMENTS

I would like to thank:

Lynne Stewart for all her help in gathering the information from the chefs and proprietors. I hope the medication is working Lynne!

Alan Donaldson, for some wonderful photography and a great deal of patience along the way.

All the team at B&W for their help and encouragement—without them this book would still be an idea in my head.

Thanks guys.

INTRODUCTION

Glasgow is now widely recognised as one of the most vibrant and innovative cities in Britain—and its restaurants have certainly played their part in establishing that reputation. With a quality and diversity that few other cities can match, Glasgow's restaurants undoubtedly owe a great deal to the talented chefs and far-sighted entrepreneurs of the past, while the chefs of today continue to encourage a whole new generation of young chefs who will carry that reputation for excellence forward into the future.

This book is a showcase of the work of Glasgow's finest chefs and best restaurants, covering the whole range from sophisticated, traditional dining to relaxed cafe style and authentic ethnic food. Each chef has selected starters, main courses and desserts which reflect the style of their particular restaurant and its menu. Many have stressed the importance of using Scottish ingredients in their recipes—something that I wholeheartedly agree with—while the variety of dishes included means that there really is something for everyone in this book.

Glasgow on a Plate is intended to encourage the reader to try out the recipes at home, but I hope it will also inspire people to venture out and experience the unrivalled possibilities for eating out that Glasgow has to offer.

FOREWORD

I am delighted to welcome you to the first edition of *Glasgow on a Plate* prepared by world-renowned chef Ferrier Richardson, whose passion for food is equalled only by his similar ardour for Glasgow. His credentials as a chef of international stature are well documented. As past manager of both the Scottish and British Culinary Olympic teams, Ferrier led his colleagues to win the Top Team award (1993), as well as a clutch of gold and silver medals.

Voted top regional UK city for the best choice and quality of its restaurants in Harden's Top UK Restaurants 1999 guide and best UK city of 1998 by readers of Conde Nast Traveller, Glasgow offers all the buzz and excitement you would expect from one of Europe's liveliest destinations—making it the perfect place for a cultural or gastronomic short break.

In keeping with Glasgow's innate sense of style and its successful reign as UK City of Architecture and Design 1999, the architectural and design features of the city's eateries are viewed as importantly as the quality of cooking and freshness of ingredients. From art deco oyster bars and fin de siècle brasseries, to art nouveau tearooms and the very latest in minimalist, millennium chic, Glasgow's restaurants cover the complete style and taste spectrum. Whatever the surroundings, however, the emphasis is always on quality and using fresh local produce including Scottish lamb, salmon and venison—perhaps washed down with a wee dram of malt whisky.

Glasgow's cafe society also gives a strong European feel and some of the best latte, mocha and espresso are served up with a well-loved, local speciality—caramel short-cake (calorific, but worth it). If world cuisine is on your agenda, you can also dine in a different country every day—from Pacific Rim and French country cooking, to Indian balti, fresh Italian pasta, and, of course, traditional Scottish fare.

I hope I have whetted your appetite and that you will enjoy not only reading about the city's outstanding chefs, but also try out some of their imaginative recipes and bring a flavour of Glasgow to your own dinner parties.

EDDIE FRIEL
Chief Executive,
Greater Glasgow and Clyde Valley
Tourist Board

Please note: all recipes serve four people
unless otherwise stated

TOM BATTERSBY

'Practically everything under the sun has already been tried, so I take classic combinations, treat them with reverence and make them as good as they can be'

At university I studied History and Sociology, and after working in sales and marketing for a few years I decided that I wanted to turn my enthusiasm for cooking into a job. So I approached Ronnie Clydesdale at the Ubiquitous Chip in search of some experience. Although I could cook I didn't know how to get thirty meals out of a kitchen in less than an hour, and that's where I learned to do it.

When we opened The Cook's Room, the dream that my wife and I shared was that the restaurant would become the friendliest place in the friendliest city and that the food would be sourced, cooked and served with passion. The restaurant itself has the feel of a really comfortable, familiar dining room, and I've made sure that The Cook's Room isn't stuffy; it's about making people feel welcome and at ease.

I know that food is not the only reason people go out for dinner, so it's important that everything is done right and to the best of our ability. We must be doing something right, as over 70% of our customers are return visitors—which is a massive compliment for any establishment to receive.

But there have been plenty of sticky situations we've had to deal with. One challenging occasion involved the loss of electrical power for a whole day. Rather than admit defeat and close, we contacted all those who had bookings to warn them that the evening would be *slightly* darker and the menu *slightly* different than usual. Surprisingly, everyone kept their reservations and, with some careful planning and strategically-placed candles, a potential disaster turned into a memorable and successful evening.

I have come to the conclusion during my time as a chef that there's nothing really new to be discovered. Practically everything under the sun has already been tried, so, rather than steal ideas, I take classic combinations, treat them with reverence and make them as good as they can be. Twists and novelties too often distract from the final dish, so I avoid them.

SCALLOPS AND A CRAB CAKE

Serves 6

24 good-sized king scallops (shell discarded, orange corals intact)

250g unsalted butter

2 red chillies

150g kale

100g streaky bacon, preferably thick-cut

2 cloves of garlic

4 spring onions

200g mixed cooked crabmeat

1 baking potato

1 egg

200ml milk

Flour

Breadcrumbs

Cayenne pepper

Scallops have a unique sweet, buttery flavour which benefits from 'unfussy' treatment, even undercooking—providing they are absolutely fresh.

Bake the potato at 200°C (Gas mark 6) for one hour or until cooked. Discard the skin and mash the potato in a bowl.

Meanwhile, finely chop the garlic and one chilli and gently fry, taking care not to let the garlic burn. Once cooked, add the finely chopped spring onions.

When this mixture and the potato have cooked, combine both with the crabmeat and add salt and a pinch of cayenne pepper. Be careful not to overwhelm the taste of the crab.

Divide the mixture into balls the size of tomatoes and flatten slightly.

Make an egg wash by mixing the egg and milk, then coat each cake thoroughly with flour, egg wash and breadcrumbs. Refrigerate.

Tear the kale from its tough stems and wash thoroughly. Bring a pan of water to the boil, remove from the heat and plunge in the kale. Leave for no more than one minute, drain and refresh under cold water—this will eliminate the bitterness but retain the colour and bite.

Clarify the butter by heating in a saucepan until melted, and allow to stand for a few minutes before pouring the clear liquid into a jug, disposing of the solids left in the bottom of the pan.

Fry the crab cakes gently in a little oil until golden brown, turning half-way through. Meanwhile, add enough clarified butter to a second frying pan to cover the surface, and place over a medium heat.

Add the scallops, in batches if necessary, and cook for one to one and a half minutes on each side, until just colouring. Remove the scallops to a warm place.

Chop the bacon into cubes about $1/2$ cm square and fry. Once cooked, stir in the kale to heat and add a good twist of black pepper.

To serve, place the kale and bacon on to plates, and top with the crab cake and a small heap of scallops. As a final touch, the remaining chilli may be cut into rings, deseeded, dipped in flour and fried until crisp, then divided amongst the plates together with a thick wedge of lemon.

TOM BATTERSBY

BLACK PUDDING AND GOATS' CHEESE

Serves 6

6 slices of black pudding

  (1 cm thick, with the skin removed)

250g goats' cheese log

6 slices of Italian bread

1 clove of garlic

Extra virgin olive oil

$^1/_2$ frisée lettuce

$^1/_2$ oak leaf lettuce

50g pine nuts

Handful of fresh basil

Raspberry vinegar

Balsamic vinegar

6 ripe plum tomatoes

Sea salt

A few fresh chives

I think this starter captures the spirit of The Cook's Room approach; robust, intensely flavoured and straightforward. The creamy richness of black pudding and goats' cheese is counterbalanced with the sharp, crisp basil and pine nut salad, and sweetened with a little raspberry vinaigrette.

Slice the tomatoes in half, vertically, and lay skin-side down in a 12-bun tray. Sprinkle each with olive oil, balsamic vinegar and sea salt, and place the tray at the bottom of a cool oven—140°C (Gas mark 1). Leave for at least an hour to caramelise and soften.

Toast the pine nuts in a tray under the grill, shaking occasionally until—literally—nut brown.

Wash and dry the lettuces and mix in a bowl with the basil leaves and the pine nuts.

For the dressing, mix one tablespoon of raspberry vinegar, three tablespoons of olive oil, add salt and pepper, and leave to infuse.

Set the black pudding slices on a baking tray and cook one side under a hot grill. Once done, turn over and top each slice with one or two rounds of goats' cheese. Return to the grill until the cheese just begins to melt, then keep warm.

Toast the bread in the usual way and once done, rub each slice on one side with raw garlic and drizzle with olive oil.

To serve, place a slice of toast, garlic-side up, on each plate and top with the black pudding and goats' cheese. Toss the salad with its dressing and place a handful on each plate. Finally, set two tomato halves on each plate and snip a few chives over the goats' cheese and tomatoes.

TOM BATTERSBY

MARINATED LAMB CHOPS
WITH ROASTED VEGETABLES

Serves 6

18 medium or 12 large lamb loin chops

Extra virgin olive oil

2 tsp dried oregano

Salt

1 head of garlic

3 lemons

2 chillies

3 red peppers

2 courgettes

1 aubergine

3 red onions

A few sprigs of fresh rosemary

500ml chicken stock

Balsamic vinegar

Clear runny honey

30g fresh Parmesan cheese

18 black olives

6 sprigs of fresh mint

For this recipe, we always use hill lamb from the Isle of Mull in autumn, as we find its depth of flavour is much improved over the traditional spring lambs.

To marinate the lamb chops, first peel the garlic and split and deseed the chillies. Roughly chop the garlic and chillies together with 2 whole lemons, combine in a bowl, then set aside.

In a separate bowl, mix 150ml olive oil with the oregano and 1 tsp salt. Take a ceramic or glass container big enough to accommodate all the chops, and dip each chop in the olive oil mixture, then lay in the container. Once the bottom is covered, add a handful of the garlic/lemon/chilli mix. Continue to build up in layers, then cover and refrigerate for at least 4 hours, and up to 24 hours.

Cut the red peppers in half and remove the seeds and stems. Place them skin-side up on a tray in the oven at 200°C (Gas mark 6). After half an hour or so, the skins will blacken and the flesh will lose its bitterness. Remove from the oven, allow to cool and then rub away the burnt skin.

Cut the onions into quarters and prod a little fresh rosemary here and there between the layers of each segment, taking care not to let them fall apart. Slice the courgettes length-ways about 4mm thick having removed top and tail. Slice the aubergine diagonally 1cm thick, and place the slices in layers in a colander over a bowl, sprinkling each layer with salt to draw out the bitter juices. After half an hour, rinse the aubergine slices and pat dry.

Lay all the vegetables, apart from the peppers, in a roasting tray, brush with olive oil, sprinkle with sea salt and set on the middle shelf of an oven at 200°C (Gas mark 6). After 15 minutes, add the peppers to the tray. Check from time to time to see that they are all cooking evenly—they should take about a further five minutes.

Meanwhile, remove the lamb chops from the marinade, discarding any little chunks of garlic, chilli and lemon. Add the chops to a large frying pan, at medium heat, and cook in batches. They will take about 5 minutes each side for 'pink'. Remove the chops to rest, and once they are all cooked, pour off any excess fat. Then, add the chicken stock to the pan, scraping up any bits stuck to the bottom. Let the sauce come to the boil and reduce a little (a thin gravy is better). Add 1 tsp balsamic vinegar, about 1 Tbsp of honey and then salt to taste.

To serve, make piles of vegetables on each plate, grate Parmesan and sprinkle a little over each pile. Then, prop the chops up against each pile, pouring over with a little gravy. Finally, add a wedge of lemon, 3 or 4 black olives and a sprig of mint. The best accompaniment to this dish is either pesto mash or rosemary and garlic roast potatoes.

DATE PUDDING*
WITH BUTTERSCOTCH SAUCE

Serves 6	300g self-raising flour
200g preserved dates	3 large eggs
1 tsp baking powder	2 tsp ground ginger
250g unsalted butter	500ml double cream
300g castor sugar	6 fresh figs

Take 6 individual or 1 large pudding basin, brush the inside with melted butter, then sprinkle thoroughly with flour, shaking away any excess.

Stone and roughly chop the dates and place in a bowl, covering with 300ml of boiling water. Add the baking powder and allow to stand.

To make the sponge, beat 200g of the butter (softened) together with 150g of castor sugar until creamy and pale. Add the eggs one by one, beating all the time. Sift the self-raising flour and ground ginger together, then fold in the sponge mixture. Lastly, add the dates with their liquor, again folding the mixture together. Divide the mixture between the pudding basins, allowing $1^{1}/_{2}$ cm for the sponges to rise, and bake at 180°C (Gas mark 4) for 25 minutes or until the tops of the puddings bounce back into shape when lightly pressed.

For a smooth, dark brown butterscotch sauce, put 150g of sugar and 500ml water into a heavy-bottomed saucepan and heat until the sugar melts. Boil vigorously until the mixture starts to caramelise. Stir continuously to prevent burning. Remove the pan from the heat until the sauce turns a chocolate brown colour. Allow to cool a little before adding 50g of butter, then slowly pour in most of the double cream. (This can be quite tricky—if the butter is added too soon, the mixture will burn; if the cream is added too quickly, the mixture will set in lumps.)

Once the puddings are done, remove from the oven and allow to stand for a few minutes. If any have risen above the rim of the bowl, cut away the excess with a bread knife so that once turned out they will stand flat on a plate.

Whip the remaining cream until it turns 'floppy'. Stand a pudding in the centre of each plate, pour over the butterscotch sauce and place a dollop of cream to the side. Finally, split 6 figs down their stems into quarters, cutting down to all but the last half centimetre so that the fig opens up but stays together. Place one on each plate and serve.

*This pudding re-heats very well if wrapped in cling-film and set in a steamer for 15 minutes, so you can cook it in advance.

ANGUS BOYD

'They say you can't teach an old dog new tricks—baloney! I'm learning from these young pups every day, even after 30 years on the stove'

Mitchells has a bistro ambience but we refuse to be categorised or pigeon-holed. Professionally we strive to create a relaxed atmosphere where our eclectic clientele can enjoy and savour their culinary experience. At Mitchell's I have always aimed to cater for three palates: everyone's grandparents, a very specific category; occasional diners and 'foodies'. It's a tall order for most young chefs when requested to prepare steak pie and lobster soufflé for the same menu—apart from a couple of exceptional cases, "never the twain shall meet".

During the course of my career I've had many great experiences, but possibly the best involved sailing around the Mediterranean and the west coast of Scotland and getting paid for it! I was employed on a privately owned yacht, catering for the family at weekends and summer trips. My boss was an unassuming type who could have been mistaken for a crew member—and was on one occasion, when he was offered a bucket of herring, "for his boss", an apology from local fishermen who had, unintentionally, jostled his yacht.

My worst experience happened while cooking for HM Queen Elizabeth on the *Maid of the Loch* on Loch Lomond, when I almost landed in hot water. Having just had my last swig of champagne I was about to launch the empty bottle into the loch when my elbow was grabbed from behind. The bottle would have sailed directly past Prince Philip's cabin window. Ironically the royal couple had been visiting the area on a 'clean up the loch' campaign.

They say you can't teach an old dog new tricks—baloney! I'm learning from these young pups every day, even after 30 years on the stove and at the front of house. It's worrying as most of them weren't even born when I started chopping onions.

I'm certainly not in this business for the money—I'm relying on winning the lottery rather than my prowess in the kitchen to make my fortune. My main aim now is to retire to a part-time position in the kitchen to give me more time on the golf course.

WEST COAST MUSSEL PEPPER POT

¹/₂ white onion

1 red onion

3 medium carrots

2 medium potatoes

2 leeks

¹/₃ savoy cabbage

75g butter

50g flour

1200ml fish stock

1800ml fresh whole mussels

300ml white wine

1 red pepper

1 green pepper

1 yellow pepper

Crème fraîche

Flat parsley

Tomato concasse

I have it on good authority that our waters are the envy of Europe and our mussel farm products are living proof of this. Mussels were once regarded as shellfish for those on a lower income bracket but now grace the finest tables across the country. This dish belies the input—simple yet stunning.

Dice all the onions, carrots, potatoes, white of the leek, green of the leek (keep separate), cabbage and peppers into medium-sized pieces.

Prepare the mussels by checking, bearding and rinsing them. (Discard any damaged or open shells.)

Make the broth by sweating off all the onions in butter without colouring. Add the carrots and cook for two minutes. Then add the flour and stir carefully for a further two minutes.

Add the fish stock (or bouillon) and potatoes, and simmer for ten minutes.

Add the white of the leek and cabbage and check for seasoning. Do not overcook.

Select a thick-based pot large enough to accommodate the broth and the mussels. Place on a fierce heat and when very hot, carefully tip the wine and mussels into the pot and cover to steam them open. Add the peppers and green of the leek and cook for one minute. Then add the hot broth and carefully mix together.

Ladle into large warm bowls, drizzle with crème fraîche, and top with flat parsley and diced tomato concasse. Serve with chunks of freshly baked or garlic bread to soak up the delicious broth.

SEARED COLLOPS OF CHICKEN
WITH ROAST GARLIC, ROOT VEGETABLES
AND A SHERRY VINEGAR BUTTER SAUCE

4 x 250g chicken supremes	16 cloves of garlic
8 turned carrots	550g butter
8 turned Scottish turnips	225g brown sugar
12 shallots	125ml sherry vinegar
8 turned potatoes	Parsley
16 red cherry tomatoes	Chervil

The first main-course dish is self-contained, requiring little in the way of side orders. Don't worry about the garlic as it has a much sweeter taste when roasted—trust me, I'm a chef!

Lightly oil the cloves of garlic and roast until the skins can be easily squeezed free.

Turn (or cut into even sizes) the carrot and turnip. In separate pots place the carrot, turnip and peeled shallots with 75g butter and 75g sugar. Add a little water to prevent burning. Blanch the potatoes until two-thirds cooked. Finely chop the parsley and chervil.

Place the carrot, turnip and shallots on the stove to cook until lightly glazed and just done, taking care not to dry out completely. Heat a large thick-bottomed pan in which place the seasoned chicken supremes with a little oil. When golden coloured, turn over, seal the other side and then add the potatoes, garlic and 75g butter.

Place in the oven to cook, at approximately 220°C (Gas mark 7). Add the cherry tomatoes 3-4 minutes before you remove the chicken from the oven.

Place the sherry vinegar in a sauté pan (preferably a tin-lined one) with a tablespoon of water and reduce by three-quarters. Take 250g of chilled butter, dice into 16 pieces and gradually whisk in the butter over a very moderate heat. Do not allow to boil.

Remove the chicken from the pan, allow to rest for two minutes but keep warm. Retain the juices from the pan.

On warm plates arrange the glazed turnip, carrot, shallots, potatoes and cherry tomatoes.

Carve the chicken into collops (thick slices) and arrange on the centre of the plate. Top with roasted garlic and spoon over the cooking juices. Drizzle around the sherry vinegar, butter and lightly sprinkle with the chopped herbs.

LAMB NOISETTES AND KUMARA PIE
WITH WHISKY PAN JUICES

12 noisettes of lamb

1 measure of whisky

600ml of lamb stock

750g of orange sweet potato (kumara)

2 medium onions (1 Spanish, 1 red)

50g butter

300ml double cream

300ml fresh soured cream

1 Tbsp of garam masala spice

$\frac{1}{2}$ tsp ground nutmeg

1 clove crushed garlic

$\frac{1}{2}$ tsp of turmeric

Coriander leaves

Chives

Seasoning

Our second main course combines succulent Scottish lamb with the more unusual sweet potato, kumara. This orange-fleshed tuberous root is often used in Creole cookery and the infusion of flavours provides a sweet accompaniment, alive with colour.

Lightly scrub the sweet potato and slice, retaining the skins.

Mix the garlic, garam masala, nutmeg, turmeric, creams, sliced onion and seasoning. Combine the potatoes with the creamy mixture and place in an earthenware dish. Lightly brush the mixture with melted butter ready for baking.

Bake the kumara potato pie in a pre-heated oven at 175°C (Gas mark 4) for approximately one hour until the potatoes are soft, golden brown and have absorbed most of the cream mixture.

Season the lamb and seal in a hot, lightly-oiled pan. Cook to the desired degree although I recommend that the meat remain pink in the middle. Remove the lamb, allow to rest and keep warm.

Deglaze the pan with the whisky, add the lamb stock and reduce by two-thirds. Check the seasoning.

Use a pastry cutter to mould the kumara pie.

Neatly arrange the lamb noisettes on a warm plate, place the kumara potato on the dish, spoon some of the cooking cream from the potatoes, and drizzle the whisky and lamb juices around the lamb. Coriander leaves and chopped chives may be used to garnish the dish.

ANGUS BOYD

GOOD OLD RHUBARB PIE
AND SAUCE ANGLAISE

900g rhubarb

175g plain flour

75g unsalted butter

150g castor sugar

1 vanilla pod

4 egg yolks

600ml milk

Ice cold water

1 whole egg, beaten

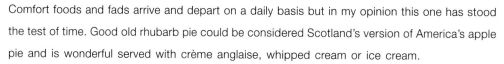

Comfort foods and fads arrive and depart on a daily basis but in my opinion this one has stood the test of time. Good old rhubarb pie could be considered Scotland's version of America's apple pie and is wonderful served with crème anglaise, whipped cream or ice cream.

Place the flour and 25g of sugar in a bowl and rub in the diced butter. When the mixture has a breadcrumb appearance gradually add the ice cold water to create a paste. Do not overmix and allow the pastry to rest for 20 minutes in the fridge.

Chop the rhubarb into large chunks.

Roll out the pastry to form a lid and use it to line a pie dish. Chill the pastry for a further 10 minutes. Lightly dampen some greaseproof paper, place on the pastry and cover with dried pulses or ceramic beans. Place the pie dish in the oven at 220°C (Gas mark 7) for 10-15 minutes.

Carefully cook the rhubarb and 75g of sugar.

Remove the beans from the pie and egg wash the pastry. Place back in the oven for a further 3 minutes to seal.

Heap the rhubarb into the dish and cover with the pastry lid. Brush the top with beaten egg and bake for approximately 30 minutes. Five minutes before the end of baking sprinkle sugar on top of the pie and bake until done.

For the sauce anglaise, put milk containing the vanilla pod on the stove to heat.

Beat the egg yolks and 50g sugar together. Just before the milk boils, remove the pan from the stove and whisk into the egg mixture. Strain the mixture back into the pan and place on a very low heat, stirring continuously for approximately 3 minutes. The consistency should remain thin, barely coating the back of the spoon. Beware! Overheating will result in scrambling.

Neatly slice the pie, place on a plate and spoon the sauce anglaise round about.

ALAN BROWN

'While still at school, my brothers and I would race home for lunch— not to eat it, but to prepare it'

Growing up in our family hotel—Auchterarder House—I was introduced to the world of catering at a fairly young age. While still at school, my brothers and I would race home for lunch—not to eat it, but to prepare it. Once, I *almost* cooked for the supermodel Linda Evangalista. She was doing a photo shoot at Auchterarder House, and when I asked what she would like me to prepare for her dinner she looked at me in horror and replied: "Oh no—nothing!! I had a fruit scone for lunch in Paris."

My father was a chef for 30 years and a perfectionist with it, and he had the greatest influence on me. I will never forget his words of advice, especially being told: "practise a dish, perfect it and then leave it, and if it's a success, don't be afraid to keep it on the menu."

I'm a bit of a traditionalist and enjoy using simple ingredients, as un-adulterated as possible. I'm also heavily influenced by Anton Mossiman and intrigued by his philosophy of 'cuisine naturale'—taking the finest ingredients and doing as little as possible to change their original characters and flavours. I've found that the best results are achieved this way, and with the amazing variety of Scottish produce available, it's a style of cooking that certainly makes our job so much easier.

During my career I've learned the importance of delegation, and the need to be adaptable and aware of what's happening in the market. But in this business the most important thing is to listen to the customer. With the third Bouzy Rouge now open in Edinburgh and the search on for other sites in the UK it seems as though we are giving the customers what they want. So far so good, but my aim now is to create something entirely different from Bouzy Rouge—a fine dining restaurant with a Michelin award.

The cuisine at Bouzy Rouge is what I call 'casual gourmet dining' appealing to different tastes and styles. The recipies I have chosen, with their simple methods, fresh local ingredients and stunning presentation, reflect this approach.

A GATEAU OF SCOTTISH PUDDINGS
SERVED WITH AN ORKNEY CHEESE SABAYON
WITH BUTTERED SHALLOTS

350g spicy haggis

350g white pudding

350g black pudding

350g of finely diced shallots

275ml double cream

2 egg yolks

225g mature Orkney Cheddar

Seasoning

Warm the puddings and layer some of each into stainless steel moulds, pressing down with a spoon.

Sauté the shallots lightly with some butter, and place on top of the puddings.

Warm the egg yolks over warm water in a stainless steel bowl, taking care not to overheat or whisk. Add the warm double cream slowly until the mixture begins to thicken. Add the grated cheese a little at a time and season to taste.

Place the puddings on a warm plate and slide off the mould. Spoon a liberal amount of sabayon around the gateau, and place under a grill or salamander until golden brown.

ALAN BROWN

MILLE FEUILLE OF
WEST COAST SCALLOPS
WITH A CREAM AND
GINGER REDUCTION

12 fresh scallops

 (ask your fishmonger to remove them from the shell)

1 small pack of filo pastry

110g unsalted butter

275ml good fish stock

A little dry white wine

Fresh double cream

1oz freshly grated ginger

Shallots

8 west coast langoustines

Remove the orange tongue from the scallops, rinse and dry. Slice each scallop into 3 and season. Open out the filo pastry, and with a 10cm round cutter cut 16 rounds.

Slowly melt the butter to clarify it. This removes the milk content and stops the butter from burning when shallow frying the filo pastry. In a shallow frying pan fry the pastry until it is golden brown on both sides. Remove from pan and drain on kitchen paper.

In a small, very hot sauté pan with no butter or oil, sear the scallops for approximately 30 seconds until golden brown on each side. Take care not to overcook.

Fry the shallots and ginger in a small amount of butter and then add the white wine. Make sure you ignite the alcohol as this will remove any bitterness. Add the fish stock and reduce until there is only a small amount of liquid left, then add the double cream. Reduce further, sieve into a clean saucepan, and add seasoning.

Bring a large saucepan of water to the boil and add the langoustines. Remove from the heat and allow to cool for five minutes.

Extract the flesh from the tails. The flesh will be used as a garnish.

On a warm plate arrange the filo pastry alternately with the 3 slices of scallops until you have formed a small tower. Spoon the ginger sauce round the plate, and place the langoustines on the top. Place under a grill to heat.

A MEDLEY OF WILD PERTHSHIRE FOWL

WITH A DEANSTON MALT WHISKY JUS

2 pigeons

2 woodcock

2 small wild ducks

225g mashed potato

225g red onions

175g fresh spinach

275ml good game or beef stock

2 measures of Deanston malt whisky

50g redcurrant jelly

2 shallots

50g unsalted butter

6 juniper berries, crushed

Remove the breasts from all of the birds.

Roast the carcasses and add 1 litre of water to make a rich game stock.

Seal all of the breasts in a shallow frying pan, lay on a baking tray and put into a resting oven or a cool oven for 15 minutes to warm through so that the flesh is still pink but the blood does not run when sliced.

Fry the shallots and crushed juniper berries, then deglaze with the malt whisky until the alcohol ignites.

Add the game stock and when this has reduced, add some redcurrant jelly. Strain through a fine sieve into a clean saucepan and bring back to the boil.

Add the unsalted butter which will improve the consistency and leave a sparkling shine on the sauce.

Boil and mash the potatoes, lightly poach the spinach and caramelise the onions.

Arrange small amounts of mashed potato, caramelised onions and spinach and place a breast on top of each.

Add the sauce, warm under the grill or salamander, and serve.

ALAN BROWN

RED WINE JELLY
WITH SOFT BLAIRGOWRIE BERRIES

550ml red wine

2 sheets of leaf gelatine

100g fresh raspberries

100g redcurrants

100g loganberries

100g strawberries

100g blackcurrants

550ml double cream

4 egg yolks

1 vanilla pod

225g castor sugar

Add 225g of castor sugar to 275ml of water, and bring to the boil to make sugar syrup. Add the red wine and gelatine to the sugar syrup and bring back to the boil. Set aside to cool.

Take individual dariole moulds and line with cellophane. Fill with a mixture of the washed and dried berries, saving some for the garnish. Cover the mixture with the cool jelly mixture and refrigerate until set.

To make the sauce anglaise, whisk the eggs over warm water in a stainless bowl, taking care not to overheat, until the eggs are creamy and light.

Add warmed double cream, castor sugar and the vanilla pod, and whisk until the sauce thickens. Strain out the vanilla pod.

Remove the jelly on to a plate and arrange some of the berries around. Add a liberal amount of sauce anglaise and serve.

STEVEN CAPUTA

'I had always wanted to be an engineer, but there were no school work placements in engineering. Cooking is much the same—except that I build food instead of building bridges'

I had always wanted to be an engineer, but there were no school work placements in engineering so I ended up at the Hospitality Inn near my home. I don't regret it—being a chef gives me great satisfaction, and seeing the raw product through to the finished article is an amazing process. In fact cooking is much the same as engineering—except that I build food instead of building bridges.

Coming to Glasgow from my small west-coast home town has had a significant effect on my life and career, allowing me to work in some excellent restaurants and learn from extremely talented chefs. They've shown me that ambition, passion, commitment and confidence are vital to cooking nice food—and that knowledge comes further down the list.

And when it all goes wrong, a little confidence can go a long way. Like the time I cooked a gourmet dinner for 30 chefs in a local restaurant. When it came to dessert, the chocolate mousses had been carefully arranged, garnished and set on trays to be carried to the tables. On her first step, the waitress tripped and somersaulted to the foot of the stairs, smashing the whole lot. Luckily, she was unhurt, but I now had two minutes to prepare a dessert for 30 impatient chefs. I hurriedly put together a botched soufflé. The disaster went unnoticed, or at least no-one mentioned it—except for some of my friends in the party who delighted in my misfortune and haven't let me forget about it ever since.

My style of cooking is fairly eclectic, but I always use the best Scottish ingredients. I don't focus my menus on one particular style of food; I look to current and past trends, classic cooking and different parts of the world—learning from them and evolving my own dishes.

TWICE-BAKED CHEDDAR SOUFFLE,
LEEK AND A LIGHT WHISKY AND HERB CREAM

Serves 6

For the Souffle:

50g butter

160ml milk

75g strong, mature Cheddar

25g Parmesan

25g breadcrumbs

100g egg white

For the garnish:

225g picked spinach

4 spears of asparagus

1 large leek

For the sauce:

50ml vegetable stock

85ml double cream

25ml white wine

1 measure Scottish whisky

1 tsp picked tarragon

1 tsp chives, chopped

1 tsp parsley, chopped

1 tsp chervil, chopped

Salt and pepper

Melt the butter in a pan over a low heat, add the flour and cook for 4 minutes, stirring continuously. Slowly add the milk until everything is incorporated. Fold in the Cheddar cheese and half the Parmesan, cool and reserve.

Whip the egg whites until soft peaks appear.

Butter six 8cm ramekins and line with the remaining Parmesan and breadcrumbs. Fold the egg whites into the cheese mixture gently, to incorporate as much air as possible. Place the mixture into the ramekins and bake at 200°C (Gas mark 6) for 8 minutes.

Blanch the asparagus until soft, remove and refresh with cold water. Blanch the spinach, remove, refresh, dry and season.

Reduce the white wine in a pan, add the vegetable stock and whisky, reduce again and add the double cream and herbs. Season to taste.

Dice and cook the leek, and season to taste. Place an amount of leek, spinach and asparagus on each plate and a single ramekin on top of each. Spoon the sauce around and serve.

RAVIOLI OF WILD MUSHROOMS,
MADEIRA REDUCTION, ROCKET AND PARMESAN

For the filling:

275g mixed wild mushrooms
  (washed and roughly picked)

100g chicken flesh

25g chopped tarragon

25ml white wine

100ml double cream

1 shallot, diced

25g butter

Salt and pepper

For the pasta*:

250g flour

7 egg yolks

3 Tbsp water

Salt and pepper

For the garnish:

50g rocket leaves

For the glaçage:

50g Parmesan

1 egg yolk

30ml double cream

In a food processor, combine all the pasta ingredients. 'Pulse' the contents briefly until just combined, but do not overwork. Remove and reserve in a fridge for one hour.

Purée the chicken flesh with the white wine, salt and pepper until smooth, then add the cream and set aside.

Sweat off the diced shallot in a pan with the butter, add the wild mushrooms and cook until soft. Remove from the pan, dry and chill in the fridge. When the shallot and mushroom mixture is cold, mix with the chicken mousse and then add tarragon, salt and pepper.

Whip double cream for glaze and when stiff add the egg yolk, Parmesan, salt and pepper.

Roll out the pasta, a little at a time, until very thin but still whole. Cut out two sizes of disc—for tops and bottoms. Place a teaspoon of the mushroom mix in the centre of each smaller (bottom) disc, and dampen with a little water.

Place the lids on each raviolo, press to close, then cut with rings.

Put the ravioli in a pot of boiling water and simmer for 6 minutes, being careful not to let the water boil.

To serve, place the ravioli on a baking tray, sprinkle a little Parmesan and glaçage (the egg yolk and cream) on top, grill and serve. Garnish with rocket leaves in the centre.

* *Special equipment required*: Pasta machine (or small flat rolling pin), 6 - 9cm round cutter.

BAKED POLENTA AND MOZZARELLA

WITH GRILLED ASPARAGUS, CRISP-FRIED CEP RISOTTO
AND OVEN-DRIED TOMATOES

400g polenta (thinly set)

20 slices of boiled potato

200g blanched spinach

1 ball of buffalo Mozzarella

20 spears asparagus

50g grated Parmesan

50g diced butter

500ml vegetable stock

100g nano risotto rice

30g ceps

2 shallots, diced

25g diced tarragon

55ml tomato coulis

55ml pesto sauce

55ml balsamic vinegar

100g fine breadcrumbs

5 large ripe plum tomatoes

30ml olive oil

Sea salt (coarse)

Skin and deseed the plum tomatoes. Brush with a little olive oil and sprinkle with sea salt. Bake in a low oven (90°C) for 2 hours, turning once. Alternatively, oven-dried tomatoes can be bought ready prepared.

Sweat the diced shallots in butter until soft, add rice and stock. Cook for 8 minutes until the mixture is left with a little bite. Add the ceps, tarragon, butter and Parmesan, and when cool, shape into small burger shapes and cover in breadcrumbs.

Split the polenta horizontally and place the bottom section on a baking tray. Top with spinach and Mozzarella, then place the other half of the polenta on top. Bake at 260°C (Gas mark 9) for about 4 minutes.

Sear the potatoes on a griddle, rotate to form a criss-cross pattern, and finish with oven-dried tomatoes.

Skewer 5 pieces of asparagus together, butter and grill.

Deep fry the risotto cakes until golden brown.

To serve, ziz-zag the tomato coulis, pesto and balsamic vinegar across large flat plates. Place the sliced baked polenta in the centre of each plate with asparagus on top. Then place slices of potato around with the risotto on top.

STEVEN CAPUTA

APPLE 'TART AU TAIN'

WITH HOUSE VANILLA ICE CREAM

For the ice cream:

150ml milk

300ml double cream

1 vanilla pod

300ml water

200g sugar

7 egg yolks

For the tart:

6 apples, peeled

775g butter puff pastry

100g brown sugar

20g butter

25g ground cinnamon

To make the ice cream, boil then simmer the milk and double cream with the split vanilla pod in a heavy-based pan for 2 minutes. Leave to cool.

Mix the eggs and sugar in a mixer to sabayon (foam) until white and 'peaky'. Add 300ml boiled water and continue to mix until thick again.

Mix with the milk and cream mixture, and rest for five minutes. Then, with a ladle, skim off any froth that may have appeared on top. Churn in an ice-cream machine until firm, and transfer to the freezer.

For the tart, peel and quarter the apples and put them in a small pan or tart case. Place on a high heat, and add the sugar and butter. Add the cinnamon and caramelise until golden brown.

Roll out the pastry into 10cm rounds about $1/2$cm thick. Cool the apple pan, then press the pastry on to the top. Sprinkle with a little extra sugar and bake for 8-12 minutes at 225°C (Gas mark 7).

Allow to cool for five minutes, then turn out on to a plate and allow to cool for another five minutes.

To serve, top with the vanilla ice cream and surround with any remaining sauce. Garnish with mint.

ANDY CHUNG

'At the Amber Regent the combination of Scottish and Chinese styles even extends to the decor—with the use of dark, Regency colours, oriental pottery and paintings of Chinese scenes by a Glasgow artist'

My training began as a child in Hong Kong where my family followed a subsistence style of living, growing and farming our own food. Even as a child I was taught about cuts of meat and fish, and the importance of fine ingredients. I still return to Hong Kong from time to time to find new ideas, as there are always things to discover in such an exciting place.

When I opened my first restaurant, The Amber, in Glasgow's West End in 1974, the image of Chinese food was changing from the days of carry-outs and chop-suey. Scottish people's tastes had developed and moved away from the takeaway Chinese and Indian culture which was so popular when I first arrived from Hong Kong over 30 years ago. At The Amber, we were quick to realise that eating habits were also changing—dining in a restaurant was no longer reserved for special occasions, but people still expected good food cooked well. We have built our reputation at the Amber Regent on the high standards which we set at the beginning—hard work, good service and quality. I think our patrons appreciate the work that goes into that and they aren't prepared to accept anything less.

One of the most important lessons I have learnt is that good preparation is vital to the smooth running of the restaurant, so we try to be ready for every situation. We have had power cuts, slightly rowdy guests and even Mick Jagger dropping in. Nothing surprises me any more—except, perhaps, when one of my golfing heroes arrives. Golf is my great love and I have my photographs, taken with Ian Woosnam and Colin Montgomerie, in pride of place in the entrance-way. If I'm not at the Amber Regent, then you'll probably find me on the golf course—especially now that after many years of long hours and late nights I've taken a back seat and passed on the day-to-day running of the restaurant to my daughter Christina.

I have always tried to raise standards of Chinese cuisine by refusing to cut corners. I still insist on the freshest seasonal produce in my restaurants—something that's vital to authentic Cantonese cooking. Scottish ingredients play an important part in the menu—sliced venison in Mandarin sauce is very popular especially with visitors from overseas and from south of the border. I have found that locally-produced ingredients give an interesting slant on traditional Chinese recipes.

At the Amber Regent the combination of Scottish and Chinese styles even extends to the decor—with the use of dark, Regency colours, Oriental pottery and paintings of Chinese scenes by a Glasgow artist. It creates a very welcoming ambience.

FRIED PORK RIBS
WITH PEPPER AND SALT

320g pork ribs

$1/2$ red chilli

1 clove garlic

$1/2$ tsp cornflour

$1/2$ tsp five spices flavours

$1/2$ tsp salt

$1/2$ tsp monosodium glutamate

$2/3$ tsp sugar

3 tsp rose-flavoured Chinese wine

$1/4$ tsp meat tenderiser

$1/2$ egg white

Clean the pork ribs with water, then chop them into 4 cm lengths.

Mix $1/2$ tsp of cornflour, $1/4$ tsp of meat tenderiser and $1/2$ egg white, and marinade the ribs for half an hour. Then mix in 2 tsp of rose favoured Chinese wine.

Heat a pan of oil and deep-fry the pork ribs until they turn brown.

Transfer the ribs to another pan, add salt, chopped red chillies, five spice flavours, sugar, chopped garlic, monosodium glutamate and wine. Stir well and serve.

LEMON CHICKEN

4 chicken breasts, skinned

Vegetable oil for deep frying

Lemon slices

2 eggs, beaten

2 Tbsp plain flour

For the sauce:

1 Tbsp cornflour

6 Tbsp cold water

3 Tbsp freshly squeezed lemon juice

2 Tbsp sweet sherry

2 Tbsp castor sugar

Coat the chicken breasts in the beaten egg, the flour, and then the egg again. Then deep-fry the chicken until golden brown.

For the sauce, heat a little oil in a wok, add all the ingredients and bring to the boil, stirring constantly. Then take the wok off the heat.

Cut the chicken lengthwise, and place the lemon slices in between the chicken pieces. Pour the sauce over and serve.

CHICKEN SATAY

225g chicken meat

1/4 cup coconut milk

For the marinade:

1/2 tsp salt

1/2 tsp curry powder

1/2 cup coconut juice

1 Tbsp sugar

2 lemon leaves

1/2 tsp pepper

Satay Sauce Dip:

2 shallots

2 garlic cloves

1/4 onion

2 red chillies

1/2 cup Satay paste

1 tsp wine

1/2 cup stock

1/2 Tbsp light soy sauce

1 tsp sugar

1/4 tsp pepper

1 tsp cornflour and water mixture

Cut the chicken meat into 2¹/₂ cm x ¹/₂ cm long strips.

Mix the marinade ingredients together and add the strips of chicken. Place in the fridge for 30 minutes.

Meanwhile, make the Satay sauce by cleaning and peeling the shallots, garlic, onion and preparing the red chillies, then blending them together into a purée.

Heat a wok, add 1 Tbsp of oil, and bring to the boil. Put in the purée and sauté until aromatic, then add the Satay paste and stir well.

Sizzle in the wine, then add the stock and seasoning ingredients. Bring to the boil once more, blend in the cornflour and water mixture, and thicken to a sauce consistency.

Take a set of bamboo sticks. Remove the chicken meat and skewer 2 or 3 strips on to each stick.

Either deep fry until cooked or brush with coconut milk and grill for 3 minutes each side until cooked.

Serve hot with the Satay sauce dip.

SCALLOP WITH ASPARAGUS

6 fresh scallops

Cornflour

225g asparagus

2 Tbsp oil

1 Tbsp shredded ginger

1 tsp sliced garlic

$1/4$ tsp salt

1 tsp wine

2 Tbsp stock

1 Tbsp light soy sauce

1 tsp sugar

$1/4$ tsp pepper

Shell and clean the scallops, rub with cornflour and slice into thin pieces.

Cut off the coarse stem and nodules of the asparagus and section into $1/2$ lengths.

Heat the wok and bring the oil to the boil. Sprinkle with the salt and sauté the ginger and garlic until aromatic.

Pour in the asparagus and stir fry briefly. Add the sliced scallops and toss well.

Sizzle the wine, and add the stock, soy sauce and seasoning. Mix thoroughly and serve.

COLIN CLYDESDALE

'The beauty about being a chef is that I can take to the hills during the week, when there's not a soul about, and wander about peacefully, discovering and picking wild produce—which is usually on the menu the next day'

I loathed and detested school and left the moment I was old enough, assuming that I would make my fortune somehow or other. When autumn came and my friends had gone on to other things I found myself bored and penniless, so I started working as a kitchen porter in my father's restaurant, the Ubiquitous Chip, where I think my presence was just about tolerated.

The beauty about being a chef is that, although I don't get weekends off, I can take to the hills during the week when there's not a soul about and wander around peacefully, discovering and picking wild produce—which is usually on the menu the next day. I'm a dedicated traveller and have tried deep-fried crickets in Thailand, Guillemot in Iceland and when in Vietnam, tasted raw pork which had been marinated for three weeks in a banana leaf.

Cooking is a full-on, stressful job but it keeps my brain busy and interested. I tend to be open and honest—to the point of not always being entirely tactful. It has been said that I'm impossible to work with and maybe that's true some of the time, but I still have staff who keep coming back for more so I can't be all bad.

I remember receiving a phone call one day from a gentleman who was coming into the restaurant that evening. He requested that additional vegetarian dishes be added to the menu, and I was happy to add another couple to the three already available. When the party arrived, Carol, my partner, relayed the message from the table that the choice of vegetarian dishes was not satisfactory. In my tactful way, I let off a string of expletives and instructions to Carol about what the difficult customer should do if he wasn't happy. At the end of my outburst, there was a terrible silence—the saloon-style half doors had allowed everyone in the restaurant to hear. As the man walked out of the restaurant, Carol just said: "I don't think I need to pass that on, you've just told him yourself."

Needless to say, the Stravaigin kitchen has full-size doors now.

It was in 1998 that Stravaigin suddenly began to draw recognition, and this was a crossroads for us. The AA award had pushed us into the 'posh' bracket which we hadn't really considered ourselves part of before—until then we had just been cooking nice food and having a great time.

SAN SEBASTIAN BACCALAU TART

225g of baccalau (salt cod)

2 medium onions, peeled and halved

1 clove

2 tsp chopped chives

2 tsp chopped parsley

Salt and pepper

300ml milk (full fat)

150ml cream

6 eggs

225g shortcrust pastry

Soak the salt cod overnight in water, changing the water at least once to remove the excess salt.

Simmer the fish in the milk, onion, clove and cream, over a low heat for about 10 minutes until the unique flavour of the baccalau has permeated the liquid.

Remove from the heat and carefully strain the milk cream mixture into a mixing bowl.* Allow it to cool thoroughly before adding the parsley, chives, salt and pepper.

Lightly whisk the eggs through the cream milk mix.

Roll out the shortcrust pastry to whatever size required (the tart can be served as individual pies or as a large flan). Place the rolled out pastry in the fridge and allow to settle. This will prevent it from shrinking in the oven.

Line a dish with the pastry, making sure that the corners of the pastry go all the way into the corners of the dish. If you wish to blind bake the pastry do so; if not, don't worry.

Pour the mixture into the pie, place in an oven at 200°C (Gas mark 6) and bake the pie for 15 minutes, or until the egg mix has risen slightly and browned.

This pie is delicious served with a fresh leaf salad dressed with a nice sharp vinaigrette.

*If you save the flesh from the cod, and remove all the skin and bone, the creamy cod flakes make the most wonderful omelettes or a very interesting variation on mashed potato.

BOUILLABAISSE
OF MIXED SCOTTISH FISH

1kg mixed fish and/or seafood

1.75kg white fish bone

 (ask your friendly

 neighbourhood fishmonger)

4 cloves garlic, unpeeled

1 small whole chilli (not too hot)

1 sprig of fresh thyme

1 sprig of fresh rosemary

2 bay leaves

$^1/_2$ star anise

12 whole peppercorns

Juice of two oranges

6 whole plum tomatoes

1 small glass of dry white wine

1 bulb fennel, roughly chopped

1 white onion

$^1/_2$ leek, roughly chopped

2 stalks of celery, roughly chopped

1 large handful of flat leaf parsley

Cold water

$^1/_2$ kg new potatoes

Owing to the variety and quality of seafood to be had around the coast of Scotland, seafood medleys have been a regular feature on the menu since we opened Stravaigin. This recipe is a semi-traditional version of an old French classic that we have 'foutered' about with in many guises over the years. Don't be put off by the number of component parts in this soup—it is seriously easy to make.

 The fish content varies according to what's available at the market each day and although three varieties is probably the minimum required, there is certainly no maximum. Some combinations may work better than others but always buy with freshness in mind. Accompanied with ultra-garlicky mayonnaise and herby croutons, this dish makes a substantial starter or a great communal main course.

 In a large pot, cover the fish bones with cold water to a depth of about 15cm, bring to the boil then immediately turn down to a simmer. Skim away any scum that forms on the surface of the water. Simmer the stock for about 20 minutes, then remove from the heat and allow to sit for one hour to allow the flavours of the fish to infuse slightly. Strain the fish stock through a sieve to remove all the lumps and bones, retaining the liquid. Discard the rest.

Clean out the pot thoroughly before pouring the fish stock back in and returning to the heat. Bring to the boil and turn down to a simmer. Skim once more before adding all the other ingredients.

Allow the soup to reduce by half, then taste and adjust the seasoning appropriately.

To cook the fish, you can either poach it in a little of the broth or, alternatively, you can pan-fry or grill it. If you have an excess of decent fish stock, use it to cook some peeled new potatoes in.

To serve the bouillabaisse, place the potatoes on the bottom of your serving dish, then arrange the cooked fish around in whatever pattern you choose. Strain the fish broth over the whole ensemble and serve immediately.

COLIN CLYDESDALE

SEARED WHATEVER TAKES YOUR FANCY

ON CHILLIED NOODLES WITH A LIGHT COCONUT GRAVY

4 x 150g portions of your choice

275g fresh egg noodles

  or 4 nests of dried noodles

  (cooked as directed and refreshed

  in a colander under cold water)

Sea salt

4 cloves of garlic, roughly chopped

6 shallots, sliced into fine rings

1 chopped chilli, as spicy as you like

4 syboes (spring onions), cut diagonally

  into $2^1/_2$ cm lengths

1 tsp chopped mint

1 dessertspoon chopped coriander

$^1/_2$ red pepper, cut into fine strips

Vegetable oil, for frying

Juice of one lime

1 $2^1/_2$ cm square of peeled

  ginger, finely sliced

2 tsp fish sauce

$^1/_4$ tsp sugar

$^1/_2$ cup coconut milk

$^1/_2$ tsp Thai green curry paste

1 stalk lemon-grass,

  cut into 1cm lengths

2 kaffir lime leaves

1 tsp chopped fresh lemon balm

Sprigs of coriander

  and mint for garnish

This 'seared whatever takes your fancy' dish is an infinitely flexible concoction. It can be prepared with fish, seared sirloin, chicken breast and duck—they all work equally well. The key to this type of cooking is to have everything prepared beforehand. Once all the chopping, squeezing and peeling has been done, it is very fast food to produce.

If you feel gung-ho enough, cook everything at once using a frying pan and a wok or, alternatively, cook the meat under the grill allowing you time to concentrate on the noodles and sauce.

For the noodles, heat your wok until it is moderately hot before adding the garlic, shallots and ginger. Stir briskly then add the pepper, spring onions and chilli, tossing together over the heat for another minute.

Add the noodles and toss once before adding half the fish sauce, lime juice, sugar and the other fresh herbs.

Toss the whole ensemble until all the component parts are properly amalgamated. This process should only take a few minutes. The only thing to check is that the meat isn't overcooking.

Test the noodles for seasoning. If they are too tart, just add a little more sugar.

Serve the noodles in the centre of four warmed serving bowls. Working very quickly, rinse the wok out with cold water and immediately return to the heat. Add a little more oil, all the time keeping an eye on the meat.

Into the warming oil, add the curry paste, lime leaves and lemon-grass. Stir the whole lot through (be wary of the seriously nippy fumes which the paste gives off) and after about one minute, add the coconut milk and the remaining fish sauce and mix thoroughly.

The sauce should go a light browny-green colour. Bring to a slight simmer but don't allow to boil or it will split and look greasy. Stir for another minute then taste for seasoning.

Serve the meat on the noodles and carefully spoon the sauce around the sides. Garnish with fresh sprigs of coriander, mint, lemon balm and chopped spring onions.

SLOW-BRAISED ARGYLLSHIRE RABBIT
IN A THICK ORIENTAL ANISE GRAVY

3 rabbits, jointed	2 medium carrots, sliced on the diagonal
1 onion, sliced finely	1 green pepper, sliced finely
2 Tbsp vegetable oil	1.2 Ltr chicken stock
2 cinnamon sticks	Juice of one orange
5 cloves of garlic, peeled whole	1 tsp orange zest
1 2½ cm square of ginger, sliced	½ cup finely chopped coriander
1 tsp five-spice powder	2 tsp oyster sauce
2 whole star anise	2 tsp fish sauce
1 tsp ground coriander	1 tsp sugar and 2 tsp cornflour,
1 small tin water chestnuts	dissolved in 1 cup of water

At Stravaigin, we have always tried to utilise the best local produce and not always the glamorous ones—for example, this recipe for slow-braised Argyllshire rabbit.

Sauté the rabbit pieces until lightly browned, then add the onion and garlic, stir through before adding the cinnamon, five-spice, anise, ginger, ground coriander, chicken stock, orange juice and zest, oyster sauce, fish sauce and the sugar and cornflour solution.

Bring to the boil and then transfer the whole lot to a casserole dish, cover and place in a medium oven.

After about 40 minutes, add the carrots, pepper and water chestnuts. Stir through and return to the oven for a further 15 minutes or until the meat is tender. If the stew is looking a little dry, add some water.

Once the stew is cooked, the meat should be melt-in-the-mouth succulent, coated in an incredibly glossy, aromatic sauce.

To finish the dish, stir through half the chopped coriander and garnish with the rest. Serve immediately with plain boiled rice.

RONNIE CLYDESDALE

'Dreich, dour and culturally presbyterian, laced with flashes of conviviality—and that's the assessment of a friend'

Like many Scottish cooks, I had no formal

training or background in catering. In many ways this worked out to my advantage, as the only rule I knew was good taste. The downside was the occasional fraught dinner as I worked out what must have been blindingly obvious to a professional chef. F. Marion McNeill's book *The Scots Kitchen* was the bible—it is an incredible book which not only provides recipes but is also a social and cultural history of Scotland.

My Granny was also a great inspiration to me. She cooked food which was quite different, and one of her favourites—a haddie roe dish that she called 'Wee Breeks'—has eluded me to this day. I also ransack the folk memory of anyone who has anything to contribute, and still get a kick out of rediscovering something old and valuable. The inventiveness of the old ways, making the most of essentially cheap food, continues to amaze me. And, of course, Granny's food is now the fashion.

I used to work in the Scottish Whisky industry, and this involved a deal of dining out. It is hard to recall how conservative dining out was in Scotland in the 60s and 70s. Flambé cooking was the thing—I can still see the flames and smell the Lea and Perrins— and while we had some fine restaurants, mostly there was just an ersatz form of French cooking on offer, and pretty boring it was too. I hate austere dining: the aim here at The Ubiquitous Chip is to be relaxed and convivial, informed but informal.

Having said that, I'm told I still give the impression of being "dreich, dour and culturally presbyterian, laced with flashes of conviviality"—and that's the assessment of a friend.

I opened the Chip in 1971 with the firm idea of bringing Scotland's endangered cuisine out of the home and into the restaurant, even to assert that Scotland had a cuisine. We had some of the best and healthiest raw materials anywhere, but nobody made any virtue of this.

The job can be enormously satisfying even though kitchens are inevitably sweaty, greasy, bloody places. At least the good ones are. In most jobs you might just get a bonus at year's end: in a kitchen the message comes straight back that the customers have loved this or that dish—it gives you a nice spring in your step.

Which is not to say there aren't occasional mishaps. One I'll never forget is the customer who inquired about 'the wee boys' room' and was given directions. Unfortunately, he turned right and out the emergency door where he met some workmen digging up the lane. After a bit of debate they told him that the nearest toilet was up Byres Road, near the library—about a quarter of a mile away. The meals were served, were returned to the kitchen, and we waited. Thirty minutes later our customer came back and was heard to say: "You know, I really expected a restaurant of this standard to have its own toilet."

We also, in the very early days, dropped a bean pot on a customer's head and were as solicitous as you can imagine—we had to be. Please, we implored, return with friends and have a meal on us. Just leave us your name. He did. His name was Mr. Ouch.

WILD SALMON CAVIAR

Portion wild salmon caviar

Measure of brandy

Sea salt

Finely diced red onion or syboes (spring onions)

Cayenne pepper

It is strange that so very few people make wild salmon caviar, preferring to buy Russian keta which is expensive and not a patch on caviar made from fresh roes. It certainly requires patience but is not at all difficult. As an added bonus, most fishmongers have no use for salmon eggs, so if you have one who deals in wild salmon, you may well get them for free.

Bring a pot of water to boiling point and remove from the heat. Put the salmon roes into the water and allow to stand for 6 to 7 minutes. The object of this is to firm the enclosing membranes making the roes easier to work with.

Remove the roes and allow to cool.

Now for the delicate part. Using a knife—and sometimes your fingers—detach the eggs from the enclosing membranes, taking care not to burst them.

Place the eggs in a glazed bowl, sprinkle with coarse sea salt and give them a measure of brandy.

Serve as they are, with buttered toast and finely sliced red onion or finely diced syboes, or with some crowdie cheese which has had a little double cream beaten in and is spiked with syboes and a little cayenne pepper.

We also use the caviar with cod, to top poached or scrambled egg and on lightly boiled duck egg.

KIPPER PATE (PASTE)

Naturally smoked fish
  (i.e. only those smoked over oak chips or peat)
Per kipper:
175g unsalted butter
Lemon juice
Pinch of cayenne pepper
Dill (for garnish)

We have used this kipper pâté or paste recipe as a starter, appetiser, savoury and spread. I have a customer who even swears by its restorative power when he has had one or two too many whiskies. We wouldn't know about that, but it is certainly a great way to eat kippers.

  Jug the kippers in boiling water for 5 minutes or place, covered, in a microwave, until perfectly cooked and the flesh separates easily from the bone. It should take about 3 minutes. I prefer the microwave method as it retains the maximum flavour of the kippers.

  Allow to cool, then skin and bone the kippers carefully and put the flesh with the softened butter, a squeeze of lemon juice and the cayenne pepper into a blender. Process until a medium texture.

  Place in ramekins, top with a sprig of dill, and seal with clarified butter which has been melted then strained through muslin to remove the solids.

  It is absolutely superb served with toast or good wholemeal bread.

TURBOT IN A GREEN PEPPERCORN AND PINE KERNEL CRUST

WITH A RED WINE AND CHOCOLATE SAUCE

6 fillets of turbot
  (about 200g each)

For the stock:
1 bottle of red wine
  (a new world Pinot Noir
  or a light Beaujolais type)
900ml water
Bouquet garni of thyme, parsley,
  bay leaf and celery top

2 red onions, sliced
6 crushed black peppercorns
1 Tbsp red wine vinegar
2 carrots, sliced
Turbot carcass of trimmings,
  head and bones
Sunflower oil

For the Topping:
175g wholewheat

& white breadcrumbs
3 Tbsp broken pine kernels
40g rinsed green peppercorns
1 Tbsp sunflower oil
Sea salt
Chopped parsley

For the sauce:
One cube Bournville dark
  or other good chocolate

I know that the sauce appears an unlikely accompaniment to white fish, but the meatiness of the turbot works wonderfully well with red wine.

To make the stock, fry the sliced red onions in a very little sunflower oil until they take on a little colour, but be careful not to burn them. Add the carrots and all the other ingredients, then bring to the boil and simmer for 30 minutes. Strain and allow to cool.

For the topping, fry the ingredients until the breadcrumbs are golden.

Make the sauce by straining the stock into a clean pot and bringing to the boil. Reduce until the sauce has achieved a coating consistency, then remove from direct heat. Beat the cube of chocolate into the hot sauce—the chocolate should lend an unctuousness to the sauce but should not overwhelm the taste.

Preheat the oven to the maximum temperature.

Pat the crumbs on top of each fillet to form a coating. Brush an oven dish lightly with oil, place the fillets on top and put uncovered in a fierce oven for 2 or 3 minutes until the fish is perfectly cooked and a crust has formed.

Pour the sauce onto serving plates and place the fillet in the middle. Garnish with samphire or fresh tarragon.

CALEDONIAN ICE-CREAM

For the praline:

100g castor sugar

3 Tbsp water

75g pinhead oatmeal which has been toasted to an even brown

For the vanilla syrup:

1 cup of vanilla sugar (sugar in which a split vanilla pod has been buried
  until the sugar takes on a pronounced vanilla flavour)

200ml water

For the ice-cream:

900ml double cream

300ml milk

This Caledonian ice-cream recipe was used by Delia Smith on TV. She described it as the most delicious ice-cream she had ever tasted.

To make the praline, bring the water and sugar to boiling point in a small pan. The sugar will dissolve and the syrup will gradually change colour. When it becomes a rich caramel colour—the crack stage—remove from the heat and stir in the toasted oatmeal. Pour out on to an oiled baking tray, leave to cool and solidify. Once it has solidified, break the praline into tiny pieces about the size of uncooked rice.

Make the vanilla syrup by bringing the flavoured sugar and water to the boil. Reduce by half and then allow to cool. Beat the vanilla syrup in a mixing bowl, add the milk, then the cream, and continue beating until it just begins to thicken. You want the consistency of Chantilly.

Fold in the praline, and put into the freezer until the ice-cream begins to set—about 30 to 40 minutes. Remove from the freezer and beat again. Transfer to a loaf tin or suitable shape, cover and freeze until ready.

To serve, dip the base and sides of the tin in hot water and turn out. Press hot, buttery fried breadcrumbs into the surface and slice like cake. It is best served with soft fruit compote or Blairgowrie soft fruit in season.

ANDREW CUMMING

'I laugh from the minute I get up in the morning and try to live life to its full capacity every day'

City Merchant

is a sturdy brasserie with dark woods and a welcoming ambience. I run a tough kitchen, but I try to make it as much fun as possible, because I think enjoyment in the kitchen is relayed onto the plates which go out. At the end of each night, we all sit down and discuss any problems—that way we don't make the same mistake twice.

I laugh from the minute I get up in the morning and try to live life to its full capacity every day. But every chef has moments that they would rather forget and I have had my fair share: such as when the dumb waiter jammed, trapping an entire table's food. I don't think I have ever prepared ten main courses so quickly. My other nightmare, which I remember very clearly, was when I realised, after carefully preparing fifty crème caramels, that I had forgotten to add any sugar. They looked perfect, had all been sent out and every one had been eaten. It must have been like eating raw egg!

I eat out as much as possible—food is fashion, just like designing clothes or producing magazines. To keep ahead of the game and, if you can, set the fashion, you need to know what everyone else is doing. I travel to London, Paris and Milan to broaden my eating experiences, but my favourite restaurants are McCallum's of Troon and Gleneagles—both in Scotland.

In Glasgow, especially, you cannot get away with placing a wee bit of food on a plate; people who eat out like to be full-up after a good meal. I always try to achieve a balance in my dishes, whatever the combination—crispiness, protein, flavour, texture.

Because I like to work seasonally and the seasons are very distinct in Scotland, I'm fascinated by gardening—by what's happening in each month. I think it gives me a better understanding, somehow, of the food which goes onto the plates.

There's always room for traditional Scottish dishes on any menu but I also like to try something a little different. Both myself and my Head Chef, Joe Anderson—my 'cooking soulmate'—are not afraid to experiment. The dishes I have chosen all reflect this, and the traditions of Scottish cuisine with fresh, local produce.

ESCALOPE OF HIGHLAND VENISON

WITH A BLACKCURRANT AND LIQUORICE JUS AND BARLEY RISOTTO

8 venison escalopes (haunch or loin)

1 Ltr beef or game stock

1 Ltr chicken stock

250g blackcurrants

1 liquorice stick

1 measure cassis

1 measure Pernod

100g butter

300g pearl barley

1 small onion

40g grated Parmesan cheese

1 stick of celery

1 medium carrot

12 button mushrooms

Reduce the beef or game stock with a liquorice stick and blackcurrants.

Beat out the venison escalopes between two sheets of cling film using a meat bat.

Peel the onion and carrot and finely chop with the celery stick. Melt the butter in a thick-bottomed pan and sweat off the carrot, onion and celery. Add the barley and then, slowly, the chicken stock, stirring occasionally.

Season the mixture and continue to stir until it becomes glutinous. Add the Parmesan cheese and keep the mixture warm. Add cassis and the Pernod to the reducing stock, and reduce until the liquid is one eighth of its original volume.

Season and pan-fry the venison in a cast iron pan. Venison is best served pink, so cook for one minute on each side.

To serve, press the risotto into a ring (a scone cutter will do), place an escalope on top and pour the reduced blackcurrant and liquorice jus over the top. Finally, garnish with cooked button mushrooms (fried in a little olive oil) and liquorice sticks.

PAN-FRIED SCALLOPS

WITH COUS-COUS AND RED DEVIL DRESSING

8-12 king scallops

120g wholemeal cous-cous

20g raisins

40g mixed diced peppers

250ml light fish stock

20g chopped chives

300ml tomato juice

200ml olive oil

Tabasco

Seasoning

1 measure Red Devil whisky

Remove the scallops from their shells using an oyster knife, and remove the muscle. Be careful to keep the orange coral intact. Slice in half, and dry the scallop meat on a paper towel.

Finely dice the peppers and raisins, and chop the chives.

To prepare the cous-cous use equal volumes of stock and cous-cous. Bring the fish stock to the boil, add the cous-cous, then stir in the chopped chives, peppers and raisins. Mix with a wooden spoon until the grains have expanded and are light and fluffy. Season to taste. Keep the cous-cous warm.

For the dressing, using a food blender mix the tomato juice, olive oil and whisky with a dash of Tabasco, seasoning to taste.

Heat a pan with 10ml of olive oil until very hot, and place the scallops face down, turning after 30 seconds. Cook the other side for another 30 seconds, and season with salt and pepper.

Pour the dressing evenly onto each plate, pack the cous-cous into a 5cm mould or a scone cutter. Place the mould on to the plate and remove. Arrange the seared scallops around the sides of the cous-cous and garnish with chopped chives.

BAKED TROON COD WITH A PESTO CRUST

WITH TOMATO AND SMOKED BACON CONCASSE

4 x 250g thick cod fillets

100g fresh basil

50g grated Parmesan cheese

Olive oil

40g pine nuts

1 clove of garlic

8 plum tomatoes

6 rashers of smoked Ayrshire bacon, thick cut

500g Ayrshire potatoes

Coriander oil

Sprigs of coriander

Remove any pin bones from the cod steaks.

Prepare the tomatoes for the concasse, crossing the bottoms with a knife and removing the stems. Blanche for 30 seconds in boiling water and refresh for 30 seconds in iced water. Remove the skin, quarter the tomatoes, remove the pips and cut the tomatoes into $^1/_2$ cm dice.

Cut the bacon into $^1/_2$ cm dice.

Place the freshly picked basil, garlic, pine nuts and Parmesan cheese into the bowl of a food processor and blend at high speed, slowly adding the olive oil until it forms a smooth paste. Breadcrumbs may be added to firm up the pesto mixture.

Cut the potatoes into barrel shapes.

Place the cod fillets onto a well-oiled baking tray, evenly spread the pesto crust right up to the edges using a palate knife. Place in a hot oven (220°C, Gas mark 7) to bake.

Sauté the diced bacon and allow to crisp, add the tomato concasse and some coriander oil, season and keep warm. In the same pan, toss the barrel potatoes, season well and place in the oven for 6 minutes.

To serve, place the pesto-crusted cod in the centre of each plate and dress with the tomato and bacon concasse. Arrange the barrel potatoes around the dish, and garnish with coriander.

CHOCOLATE MOUSSE
WITH A DUNDEE MARMALADE SAUCE

125g bitter dark chocolate

125ml double cream

3 eggs

25g butter

100g castor sugar

1 sheet of gelatine

5ml vanilla essence

1 measure of brandy

Dundee marmalade

Whisky (optional)

Melt the chocolate and butter together in a bowl over a Bain Marie.

Lightly whip the cream, separate the eggs, and lightly whip the egg whites with half of the sugar to form a light meringue.

Lightly whip the egg yolks and remainder of the sugar.

Flambée the brandy and vanilla essence. Add the dissolved gelatine, then add the melted chocolate using a spatula. Mix into the yolk and sugar mixture, and fold in the light meringue.

Finally, fold through the whipped cream, pour into a timbale mould or pudding basin, and allow to set for one hour in the fridge.

Thin some Dundee marmalade in a pan over a low heat with a $^1/_4$ cup of water (adding whisky if desired) to make a sauce.

To serve, turn the mousse out onto a plate and pour the marmalade sauce round.

ANDREW FAIRLIE

'Cooking is what I do best and I am passionate about it—I hope that shows in the food here at One Devonshire Gardens'

My love of cooking

stemmed, in part, from my mother's inability in the kitchen. I remember one particular occasion when my brothers, sisters and I complained that our menu at home was too boring. In an effort to appease us, she attempted a bold new recipe—fish poached in wine. Unfortunately, she didn't have any wine so she used wine vinegar instead—with disastrous and completely inedible results. It put me off fish for years and years.

I would say that most of my jobs as a chef have been positive experiences—with the exception of my time at the Hotel de Crillon in Paris where I began my 'military service'. I'll never know how I got through those first few months of pure abuse; I don't know if they were trying me out, but I was determined, come hell or high water, to stick it out. Somehow I survived, and every other job I've had has seemed easy after that.

A total contrast to Paris, and one of the highlights of my career so far, was winning the Roux scholarship to work with Michel Guérard in the South of France. It was utterly inspirational. Michel himself was incredibly enthusiastic in his love for food—even down to the herbs he used, which he grew himself.

La Caprice in London is possibly the restaurant which I respect most—it is consistently brilliant with stylish food and menus. But we have some great chefs here in Scotland, and Hilary Brown at La Potiniere is one who I particularly admire. She is self-taught and her menus are set, simple and cooked to perfection—virtues that every chef should aspire to.

Cooking is what I do best and I am passionate about it—I hope that shows in the food here at One Devonshire Gardens. As for the future, my aim is to own, eventually, a restaurant in Glasgow. I enjoy this city and I am sure there's room for at least one more good restaurant here. I hope that will be mine.

WEST COAST FISH SOUP
WITH ROUILLE

1kg mixed west coast fish (small monkfish, small dory, red gurnend, grey mullet)	400g tinned tomatoes	3 Ltr good fish stock
	1 bunch fresh tarragon	Salt and pepper
	4 sprigs of thyme	
1 head of garlic	1 bay leaf	
100g fennel, sliced	4 parsley stalks	*For the Rouille:*
100g leeks, sliced	1g saffron threads	250g potatoes
100g carrots, sliced	6 star anise	1 clove of garlic
50g celery, sliced	50g tomato purée	3 hard-boiled eggs
150g onions, sliced	100ml olive oil	250ml extra virgin olive oil
300g fresh tomatoes, sliced	200ml white wine	Pinch of saffron
		Salt and pepper to taste

Cut the fish into pieces (including the heads etc.), wash thoroughly in cold water and drain.

In a large saucepan, heat half of the olive oil and fry the fish for 5 minutes, then add the tomato purée and cook for 2 minutes. Add the white wine, boil and remove from the saucepan.

Reheat the saucepan, add the remaining 50ml of olive oil and add the sliced vegetables, garlic and saffron, and fry over a medium heat until soft. Season to taste.

Put the fish back into the saucepan with the vegetables, cover with fish stock and add the tinned tomatoes. Bring the mixture to the boil and skim. Add the anise and herbs and simmer for one hour.

Pour the contents of the pan, in batches, into a food processor, and blend until completely smooth. Pass the soup through a conical sieve and squeeze the maximum amount of liquid through the sieve.

For the rouille: peel and quarter the potatoes, and boil in salted water until cooked. Drain and dry slightly. Crush the garlic with a little salt and place in a stainless steel bowl. Pass the potato and egg yolk through a fine mesh sieve and mix with the garlic. Add the saffron and beat the olive oil into the potato mixture a little at a time until it is all incorporated. Season with salt and pepper.

Reheat the soup, check the seasoning and serve the rouille in a small sauce boat.

ANDREW FAIRLIE

ROASTED SCALLOPS
AND STIR-FRIED VEGETABLES
WITH THAI CURRY SAUCE
AND RED PEPPER SALSA

12 medium scallops

100g mangetout

100g carrots

100g beansprouts

50g ginger

2 pak choi leaves

1 handful of red chard

For the Thai Curry Sauce:

4 medium shallots, chopped

2 cloves of garlic, crushed

2 Tbsp fresh curry paste

100ml double cream

250ml scallop stock

12 coriander leaves, chopped

25g butter

Salt and pepper

For the Curry Paste:

1 red pepper

3 green peppers

75g ginger, peeled

6 cloves of garlic

3 stalks of lemon-grass

6 tsp turmeric

2 tsp ground cinnamon

6 tsp ground cardamon

6 tsp ginger powder

2 tsp cayenne pepper

$^1/_2$ tsp English mustard powder

For the Red Pepper Salsa:

1 red pepper, roasted and peeled

1 clove of garlic, peeled

15g of ginger, peeled

1 Tbsp roasted sesame seeds

2 Tbsp rice vinegar

Juice from $^1/_2$ lime

45ml sesame oil

75ml olive oil

To make the stir fry, cut the carrots, mangetout and ginger into julienne. Heat a little vegetable oil in a wok and add the carrots. After 30 seconds, add the beansprouts, mangetout and the ginger, and cook for a further 30 seconds.

Add the torn pak choi leaves and red chard, cook for a further 30 seconds and season to taste.

For the Thai curry sauce: sweat the shallots and garlic in butter until soft and then add curry paste and cook for 2 to 3 minutes. Add the scallop stock and reduce by half. Add the cream, cook for 5 minutes, then add the chopped coriander leaves. Season and blitz quickly with a hand blender and pass through a fine sieve.

To make the fresh curry paste: blitz the pepper, ginger and garlic cloves with a little olive oil and cook gently for 20 minutes. Chop the lemon-grass and add to the pepper mixture and cook for a further 10 minutes. Add the ground spices, cook very gently for 10 more minutes and pass through a fine mesh or drum sieve. The paste may be stored in an airtight jar for up to one week, or frozen.

To make the red pepper salsa: cut the roasted and cleaned pepper into small dice and place in a stainless steel bowl. Purée the garlic, dice the ginger, then add these along with the sesame seeds and the liquid ingredients to the bowl. Whisk together and leave to marinate for 24 hours.

To serve, sear the scallops in a non-stick pan thinly-coated with vegetable oil for 45 seconds on both sides until golden brown. Spoon the stir-fried vegetables on to the centre of each plate, spoon the curry sauce around and drizzle the salsa on to the sauce. Finally, place 3 scallops onto each pile of vegetables.

STUFFED LEG AND SADDLE OF RABBIT

WITH WILD MUSHROOMS, TRUFFLE POTATO PUREE
AND BABY SPRING VEGETABLES

One rabbit, jointed

Salt and pepper

Cooking oil

300g wild mushrooms
  (Cepes, Griolles & Trompette)

1 shallot, chopped

$1/2$ clove garlic, crushed

25g flat parsley, chopped

120g pig's caul
  (soaked overnight in cold water)

25g butter

For the Chicken Mousse:

$1^1/_2$ chicken breasts

400ml double cream

1 egg white

Salt and pepper

For the sauce:

$2^1/_2$ Ltrs of brown chicken stock

1 onion

1 carrot

1 leek

1 celery stalk

1 sprig thyme

1 bay leaf

$1/2$ head of garlic

For the Potato Purée:

300g potatoes, peeled and quartered

100ml double cream

150g unsalted butter

50g chopped fresh black truffle

Cut the chicken breasts into pieces and blend into a food processor with the egg white. Pass the meat through a fine mesh sieve and place into a bowl set over ice. Season with salt and pepper and gradually add the cream, beating vigorously with a spatula until all the cream is incorporated.

Wipe the wild mushrooms free of any dirt, heat a thick-bottomed frying pan with a little vegetable oil and sauté the mushrooms for two minutes then drain them in a colander. Reheat the pan, melt the butter and quickly cook the shallots and garlic, add the mushrooms, season and cook for five minutes. Drain again and leave to cool, then add with the chopped parsley to the chicken mousse. Refrigerate until needed.

Remove all sinews from the rabbit leg and saddle meat, and carefully remove the fillets from the saddle. With a sharp knife, remove the bones from the rabbit legs.

Place the legs between two sheets of cling-film and beat with a heavy meat bat until 5mm thick, taking care not to tear the cling-film. Trim the edges of each leg so that a rectangle of approximately 14cm x 10cm is formed. Season the rabbit fillets and fry in hot fat, keeping the fillets very rare, then set aside to cool.

Season the leg meat and spoon the chicken mousse mixture down the centre of each leg. Push a rabbit fillet on to the mousse and cover with more mousse. Fold the leg meat over the mousse and fillet so that it is completely covered.

Spread the pig's caul on to a clean table. Wrap each leg up tightly in the caul and tie with string. Refrigerate for one hour.

To make the sauce: chop the remaining rabbit bones and trimmings and brown in a heavy pan for 7 to 8 minutes, remove from the pan and put the roughly chopped vegetables into the pan and brown. Place the bones into a saucepan, cover with the chicken stock, add the herbs and vegetables and bring to the boil. Simmer gently for 1$\frac{1}{2}$ hours then strain the stock and reduce by two-thirds.

To make the potato purée: boil the potatoes in salted water until completely cooked. Drain and pass through a fine sieve, then return to a clean pan. Boil 25ml of cream and add the chopped truffle. Set aside. Gradually add the remaining cream to the potatoes over a gentle heat, then beat in the butter a little at a time until the potato is silky smooth. Finally add the truffle and season to taste.

Preheat the oven to Gas mark 7 (220°C). Shallow-fry the rabbit legs, turning in the pan until they are golden brown, then place in the oven to roast for 20 minutes, turning and basting the legs at regular intervals. Remove from the oven and rest for 10 minutes. Slice each rabbit leg into six thick slices, using three slices per portion. Strain and season the reduced sauce.

To serve, place a spoonful of potato purée on the centre of each large plate. Place a rabbit leg on top of each, pour the sauce around and garnish with baby spring vegetables and young spinach leaves.

ICED VANILLA PARFAIT

WITH ROASTED STRAWBERRIES AND WHISKY

Parfait:

4 egg yolks

125g sugar

400g whipping cream

3 vanilla pods

1 gelatine leaf

Jaconde sponge base:

100g icing sugar

100g ground almonds

2 whole eggs

3 egg whites

25g flour

15g castor sugar

20g melted butter

Roasted strawberries:

20 strawberries

40g castor sugar

3 Tbsp whisky

4 Tbsp coulis

Coulis:

150ml red wine

45g castor sugar

150g strawberries

Dried strawberries:

6 strawberries

25g icing sugar to dust

For the parfait: split the vanilla pods and scrape out the seeds. Place the seeds and pods into a saucepan, add the sugar, gelatine and a little water to melt the sugar. Slowly bring water and sugar to the boil and continue boiling until syrup reaches 120°C. Remove the vanilla pods. Place the yolks into a mixing bowl and whisk on high speed, gradually pouring the hot vanilla syrup mixture on to the yolks. Whisk until almost cold by which point the yolks will have trebled in volume, and then fold in the lightly whipped cream.

For the sponge base: sieve the ground almonds and icing sugar into a bowl, add the whole eggs and beat until a ribbon consistency is achieved. Whisk the egg whites until stiff, add 15g of castor sugar and beat until very firm. Fold in the flour and melted butter to the whole egg mix and then fold in the whites. Spread the mix 6mm thick on to a greased baking sheet and bake at 250°C (Gas Mark 10) for 3 to 4 minutes. Remove and place on a wire rack to cool.

For the strawberry coulis: boil the red wine, sugar and 30g of strawberries, and reduce by half. Pour this syrup over the remaining 120g of strawberries, blend and pass through a conical sieve.

For roasted strawberries: Boil the whisky and sugar together to make a light caramel, add the 20 strawberries and turn over in the caramel with a wooden spatula. Reduce the heat and add the coulis, cook gently for 2 minutes until the caramel has melted into a deep red sauce.

For the top of the parfait, make dried strawberries by finely slicing the strawberries then laying them on a baking tray, sprinkle them with icing sugar and allowing them to dry out overnight in a warm oven (about Gas mark 2 or 150°C).

Place four stainless steel circles 40mm high x 65mm wide onto a tray lined with greaseproof paper. Pipe the parfait mix into the moulds to form a base, then pipe the mix around the edge of the moulds, leaving an empty space in the middle. Put the moulds into the freezer for two hours to stiffen up. Remove the moulds and pour some of the strawberry coulis into the centre of the parfait.

Cut out four rounds of jaconde sponge, 65mm wide, and place one on top of each mould. Replace in the freezer until ready to serve.

To serve, gently heat the moulds with your hands and tip onto the centre of four plates, sponge-side down. Garnish the top of each parfait with the dried sliced strawberries, spoon the warm, roasted strawberries and drizzle the warm sauce around the parfaits. Garnish with a mint leaf.

SANDRO GIOVANAZZI

'I was very flattered when a visiting group of Italian engineers ate here twice a day for their entire two-week stay in Glasgow. You can't get much higher praise than that'

Although I was born and raised in Glasgow, I still consider myself Italian and a little bit Scottish. I studied History of Fine Art, Italian Language and Literature at Glasgow University, but cooking has always been the family tradition. My grandfather came to Glasgow before the First World War, and while here he learned to be a fish fryer. My grandmother grew up in the tradition of the 'Osteria', the original restaurants of Italy. These restaurants served the purpose of catering for people away from home, as in those days people would only 'eat out' out of necessity. Italians also believed that their own women at home could cook as well as any restaurant cook. Italy is a nation with 5 million chefs, 95% of these being housewives, so the 'Osterie' had to be good. My father was introduced to the fish frying trade, my mother is also Italian and an accomplished cook, and when I came along I became the third generation in the catering tradition.

When my father opened La Parmigiana in 1978, there were many Italian Restaurants in Glasgow but just not many good ones. I started working for him as commis chef, peeling onions and eventually working my way up, and I still cook nearly every day. From the very beginning it has been my ambition to create genuine Italian cooking in an Italian setting, and I think we have achieved that here at La Parmigiana. I was very flattered when a visiting group of Italian engineers ate here twice a day for their entire two-week stay in Glasgow. You can't get much higher praise than that.

I have always enjoyed the countryside, ever since I was a young boy and my father and I would hunt for wild mushrooms. I now know a lot about mushrooms, but don't ask me where my hunting ground is—mushroom-hunting is an Italian's best kept secret. I also enjoy other country pursuits such as game shooting, fishing, and collecting wild berries and fruits, of which there is an abundance in the woods of Scotland. These interests have greatly influenced my cooking at La Parmigiana.

My grandfather's philosophy, which was passed to my father and so to me, is to be the best in what you do. By using the best ingredients available and the knowledge and expertise based on the traditional regional cuisine of Emilia-Romagna—more particularly, the Cucina Parmense, handed down from my mother and grand-mother—I believe that I am fulfilling that ideal, and that it is the reason for our success today. In the future, I just hope to carry on cooking great Italian food.

TERRINE OF ROASTED RED PEPPERS
AND SPINACH WITH BAGNA CAUDA

6 large red peppers

1 small bunch of spinach

3 leaves of gelatine

200g butter

1 small tin of anchovies

5 cloves of garlic

100ml olive oil

250ml cream

I am very aware of upholding the traditions of Italian food and the following recipes reflect that. Bagna Cauda, a rich sauce native to the Piedmont area of Italy, together with roasted peppers, gives an excellent marriage of flavours.

Roast the peppers under a hot grill until the skins blacken. Leave to cool.

Remove the stalks from the spinach, and blanch the leaves in boiling water.

Remove burnt skin from the cooled peppers, open and remove seeds, then quarter lengthways and pat dry.

Dissolve the leaves of gelatine in 200ml of water and line a terrine mould with spinach leaves that have been dipped in gelatine. Arrange the pepper pieces dipped in gelatine in layers in the mould. Halfway up cover with another layer of spinach then the rest of the peppers. Cover the top with another layer of spinach and refrigerate for four hours.

To make the Bagna Cauda, heat oil in a saucepan, add the anchovies and gently dissolve. Add the cream, butter and garlic cloves, heat and stir. When a thick sauce is formed, pass through a fine sieve.

Turn out the terrine by dipping in hot water for five seconds, and then invert on to a plate.

To serve, place a slice of terrine on a plate and spoon some of the sauce round it. Garnish with a sprig of basil.

TAGLIOLINI WITH SALMON AND WHISKY

400g flour

2 Tbsp olive oil

3 whole eggs and one egg yolk

200g salmon, cut into 1cm cubes

Pinch of black pepper

1/2 onion, finely chopped

250ml cream

4 Tbsp Parmesan cheese

75g butter

Measure of whisky

Although pasta was traditionally the staple diet in Italy, it is now more commonly eaten as a starter or accompaniment to much finer foods such as truffles or salmon with whisky.

Mix the flour, all the eggs, and the olive oil, kneading into a smooth dough. Set aside in a fridge for one hour.

Roll out the dough until it is very fine, flour and leave to rest for 15 minutes.

Carefully roll the dough on to itself like a Swiss roll and, with a sharp knife, cut it into 1/2 cm slices. Unroll the slices and you have your tagliolini. These can be used immediately or set aside to dry for use the next day.

Gently fry the onion in butter, then add the salmon, taking care it doesn't burn. Add the cream and Parmesan, bring to the boil and season. Keep warm.

Bring a large pot of salted water to the boil, add the pasta and cook for about two minutes (if the pasta has been left overnight it may need to be cooked a little longer). Drain when still al dente and add to the sauce.

Add the whisky, mix well, plate and serve.

OVEN-BAKED SEA BASS
WITH SLICED POTATOES

4 sea bass (up to 500g), washed, gutted and scaled

4 potatoes, very finely sliced

4 bay leaves

1 pinch of salt

1 pinch of pepper

100ml of white wine

Juice of $\frac{1}{2}$ lemon

Olive oil

Knob of butter

Handful of chopped parsley

We have an exceptional selection of fish in Scotland and sea bass is one of my favourites in terms of taste and availability. This recipe is easily prepared but is still full of flavour.

Make 3 parallel cuts in the side of the fish that will be facing upwards, place a bay leaf in each cavity and season well.

Oil the fish, place on a roasting tray, and spread the finely sliced potatoes around. Sprinkle the potatoes with olive oil and season.

Place into a pre-heated oven at 230°C (gas mark 8). After 15 minutes, pour wine onto the fish and replace in the oven.

When the fish is cooked, after about 20 minutes, pour the cooking juices into a hot pan, bring to the boil and add lemon juice and butter. Glaze and pour over the fish with a sprinkling of parsley.

PEARS POACHED IN VIN SANTO
AND SERVED WITH MASCARPONE

4 Williams pears (medium sized and ready for eating)

500ml Vin Santo

50g castor sugar

1 vanilla pod, split

Lemon juice

1 small tub of Mascarpone

In a small saucepan, bring the Vin Santo, sugar, vanilla and lemon juice to the boil.

Meanwhile, peel the pears, cut off the bottom so they will sit nicely in the pan, and wash in cold water.

Place the pears into the syrup and poach for about 20 minutes (more or less, depending on the ripeness of the pears).

Leave to cool in the syrup.

When cool, serve with a quinelle of Mascarpone.

To serve, quarter the pear lengthwise and carefully cut out the core. Arrange on a plate with the narrow ends meeting at the centre of the plate, giving you the four points of the compass with the broad ends. Place a teaspoon of mascarpone between each slice of pear and garnish with a sprig of mint at the centre.

SEUMAS MACINNES

'at the very beginning, I always imagined what it would be like to own such a beautiful restaurant'

Cafe Gandolfi is a blend between a traditional Glasgow tea-room and a continental-style restaurant, with solid sculpted wooden furniture and stained glass windows. It's a welcoming environment, and I like to think it reflects my own passion and warmth.

When I started working here—it all seems terribly long ago—I used to imagine what it would be like to own such a beautiful restaurant. Now, having reached this stage, I feel very privileged.

My first position was with an industrial catering company. Then I decided to start my own catering business—but money was so tight I had to find some extra income. That's how I started in the kitchen here at Cafe Gandolfi, peeling carrots, just to make ends meet.

From those early days as the kitchen porter, I went on to spend five years as the manager, after which I became a partner in the business for another five years. In 1996 I became the owner.

What I consider important is that the staff actually care about Cafe Gandolfi. And it goes deeper than that—it's not about me or the place, but about 'us' as a team. I think that's why we have some of the longest-standing staff in Glasgow restaurants.

Without a doubt, the very best part of it all is my family, and the sense of security which having them around gives me.

I don't have ambitions to take over the world; one thing I would like to do, though, is to write my own cookery book—if I ever get the time.

FRESH SALMON AND LEMON TERRINE
WITH DILL AND GREEN PEPPERCORNS

Serves 6

350g fresh skinless salmon

1 level dessertspoon fresh green peppercorns

1 Tbsp fresh, chopped dill

1 large lemon (or 2 small lemons)

175g unsalted butter

Salt

Segment the lemon, portioning all the pith. Do this over a bowl and collect all the juices as the segments fall.

Pick out all of the segments and dice them, discarding the pips.

Melt 100g of the butter in a large, shallow pan and as it froths, add the salmon.

Reduce the heat and continue to cook until the salmon is still transparent in the middle.

Remove from heat and leave the salmon to finish cooking as it sits in the pan. Season the fish with a generous amount of salt.

Drain and crush the green peppercorns and add them, along with the lemon flesh and chopped dill, to the salmon.

Pack the mixture into a 750ml (1.3 pint) capacity terrine, and once it has cooled place in the fridge to allow the butter to set.

Melt the remaining butter, and spoon over the terrine to seal it. Finally, sprinkle a few sprigs of dill on top and they will set in the melted butter.

CHICKEN WITH COCONUT CHILLI SAUCE
WITH PICKLED CUCUMBER AND CHILLI JAM

Serves 6

6 free range chicken breasts

For the marinade:
125ml olive oil
230ml Thai fish sauce

For the jam:
4 slices ginger, roughly chopped
1kg red chillies, seeded and finely sliced
Juice of 2 lemons
1kg white granulated sugar
Thai fish sauce

For the coconut sauce:
10 cloves garlic, crushed
6 fresh chillies, seeded and chopped
3 tsp sugar
125ml rice or white wine vinegar
125ml Thai fish sauce
600ml coconut milk
500ml olive oil
1 bunch fresh coriander, chopped

For the pickled cucumber:
1 cucumber, peeled lengthways
3 Tbsp granulated sugar
125ml white wine vinegar

Place the chicken breasts in the marinade and leave for a few hours, or preferably overnight.

The chilli jam can be stored in sterilised jars for months, but is so good it will never last that long—its uses are endless. To make the jam, put the chillies, ginger, lemon juice and sugar in a saucepan and cook over a low heat, stirring until the sugar melts. Bring to the boil and continue to cook until the jam thickens. Allow to cool before adding the fish sauce to taste.

For the sauce, place the garlic, chillies and sugar in a food processor and process until finely chopped. Add the vinegar, 125ml of fish sauce and the coconut milk, and blend until smooth. With the motor still running, quickly add the oil. Transfer the mixture to a saucepan and cook until heated—do not allow to boil. Add the chopped coriander and set aside.

For the pickled cucumber, mix the sugar and vinegar together and add the strips of cucumber.

Heat 2 Tbsp of olive oil in a large frying pan and cook chicken until it is lightly browned and cooked through. Serve the chicken on a bed of steamed rice, spooning the sauce and jam alternately around the plate.

GRATIN OF TIGER PRAWNS
WITH CHILLI AND CHEESE

200g raw tiger prawns

2-3 chopped spring onions

2 cloves crushed garlic

2 fresh red chillies, deseeded and finely chopped

280ml double cream

75g grated Gruyère cheese

Juice of 1 lime

Tabasco

Salt and pepper

Place the prawns in a bowl with the Tabasco and the lime juice.

At this point put your grill on its highest setting. Divide the garlic, chillies and spring onions into 4 ramekins, and then place the drained prawns on top.

Season everything and top with the double cream and Gruyère cheese. Put the ramekins on a baking tray and place under the grill for 5 minutes until the prawns are pink and the cheese is golden brown.

Serve with some good quality bread, and perhaps a salad.

CHOCOLATE AND WHISKY TART
WITH ESPRESSO CRUST

2 tsp (heaped) ground coffee

200g plain flour, sifted

50g castor sugar

95g unsalted butter, chilled and diced

1 large egg

300ml double cream

295g plain chocolate, roughly chopped

2-3 Tbsp whisky

Place the ground coffee, flour, sugar and butter in a food processor and mix until it resembles breadcrumbs. With the machine running add the egg and $1/2$ Tbsp cold water.

Wrap the pastry in clingfilm and put in the fridge for two hours.

Roll out the pastry and line a loose bottomed tart tin (24cm diameter, 3cm depth). Prick the pastry and leave wrapped in clingfilm in the fridge overnight.

Bake the pastry blind, using ceramic beans, for 15 minutes (gas Mark 5, 190°C) and allow to cool. Remove the beans and cook for a further 10 minutes.

Simmer the cream in a heavy saucepan, removing from the heat as soon as any bubbles appear. Stir in the chocolate, which will melt, and add the whisky. Leave to cool for 30 minutes, stirring occasionally, then pour into the pastry case. Leave to set in the fridge for at least 2 hours.

Allow the tart to come to room temperature, and serve with pouring cream.

GARY MACLEAN

'I used to watch people coming in and out of the hotels where I worked and realised that to be successful like a lot of those I was cooking for, I had to be the best and take no short cuts'

As a young chef I used to watch people coming in and out of the hotels where I worked and realised that to be successful like a lot of those I was cooking for, I had to be the best and take no short cuts. Now things seem to have come full circle, and I have been involved as a trainer for the Scottish School of Excellence, introducing children to the catering industry, following the food from suppliers and processors to the finished plated product. The scheme was a real success, increasing the children's confidence and even having a positive effect on their school grades. I'm probably proudest of one boy in particular whose headmaster said he had changed almost overnight from a "nightmare pupil" and a "rogue" into a "model pupil with a real chance". That boy is now working at Yes.

I thought I had accomplished everything I wanted, but goalposts move and priorities change. I'm a dad now, so that's shifted things and my outlook is different, but I still love being a chef and in control of my own future. With success come new challenges, and some really special moments. At the official opening of Glasgow's Gallery of Modern Art where I was executive chef, the Queen and Prince Philip were introduced to the staff in the traditional line-up. I was, of course, in full chef's regalia and Prince Philip, who I believe is known for his dry wit, said: "I suppose you're the tea boy?" He then asked if the food was 'arty' and if not, suggested that I should be sent up to the art school. I replied "No, you send them down to me." I only learnt later that it is against protocol to answer back like that, but he didn't seem too bothered by a little bit of cheek.

The food here at Yes is Northern Italian with a modern theme—healthy, very fresh and simple. The recipies I have selected highlight this theme and the wide variety of textures and flavours that can be achieved. And when it comes to cooking, flavour is everything.

SEARED MAIZE-FED CHICKEN
WITH FRIED MOZZARELLA,
TOMATO CHUTNEY AND BABY COURGETTES

2 maize-fed chicken breasts

1 packet of basil

1 ball of Buffalo Mozzarella

50g fresh breadcrumbs

1 egg

50g flour

6 plum tomatoes

25ml balsamic vinegar

$1/2$ red onion

$1/2$ red bell pepper

25g castor sugar

8 baby courgettes

Salt and pepper

Trim the chicken breasts of all the fat and excess skin. Stuff some basil under the skin and season with salt and pepper. Trim and cut the Mozzarella into 8 small circles. Dip the cheese into the flour, then the beaten egg, and finally into the breadcrumbs.

Pan-fry the chicken breast until it is crisp and golden brown, then put into a hot oven (200°C, Gas Mark 6) for 10 minutes until firm to the touch.

For the chutney, quarter and de-seed the tomatoes. Dice the tomatoes, red peppers and onion. Place the sugar and balsamic vinegar in a pan, reduce by half, then add the onion and pepper and cook for a further 2 minutes. Add the tomatoes and remove from the heat.

Halve the courgettes and sear in a hot pan. Remove and keep warm. Fry the Mozzarella in a shallow frying pan until golden brown. Remove and keep warm.

To serve, place a tidy spoonful of chutney in the centre of the plate, then fan two slices of Mozzarella at the side of the chutney. Slice the chicken and place four slices on top of the chutney and Mozzarella. To finish off, assemble the sliced courgettes on top of the chicken.

RISOTTO OF WILD MUSHROOMS AND ASPARAGUS

WITH SEARED MARINATED VEGETABLES

100g Scottish mixed wild mushrooms

750g medium flat field mushrooms,
 thickly sliced

7 Tbsp olive oil

3 garlic cloves, peeled and sliced

2 Tbsp chopped fresh basil

1 lemon

1 Ltr chicken stock

150g butter (at room temp.)

1 red onion

275g risotto rice

70ml extra dry Vermouth, white

175g Parmesan, freshly grated

12 large spears of asparagus

Heat 4 Tbsp of the olive oil in a large, heavy frying pan until smoking. Add the sliced fresh field mushrooms and fry, stirring constantly for 15 to 20 minutes or until the mushrooms have become very dark. Remove and keep warm.

Wipe clean the frying pan, heat another tablespoon of olive oil and gently fry the wild mushrooms with the sliced garlic. When the garlic begins to colour, add the other cooked mushrooms, season with salt and pepper, and stir to combine the flavours. Add the freshly chopped basil and the juice from the lemon.

Heat the chicken stock, and add seasoning if necessary.

Melt half of the butter and the remaining olive oil in a frying pan and gently fry the onion until it becomes soft. Take the pan off the heat and add the rice until the rice has become totally coated. (This should only take a minute.)

Return the pan to the heat, add two ladles of the hot stock and simmer, stirring until the rice has absorbed nearly all of the liquid. Continue to add more liquid as each amount is absorbed. After about 15 to 20 minutes, nearly all of the stock will be absorbed by the rice and each grain will have a creamy coating but remain al dente. Add the remaining butter in small pieces, then the mushrooms, Vermouth and Parmesan.

Prepare the asparagus spears for a garnish by sharpening the bottoms to a point and blanching in boiling water for 3 minutes. Drain and refresh them in ice water, and reserve. When serving, grill with salt and pepper and arrange around the risotto, in alternate directions.

PAN-FRIED MONKFISH AND KING PRAWNS

WITH LINGUINI AND BELL PEPPER DRESSING

500g diced monkfish tails

16 king prawns

8 large sprigs of rosemary

1 lemon

250g linguini pasta

50g tomato concasse

125ml olive oil

1 red pepper

1 green pepper

1 red chilli

6 black olives

1 bunch of chives

Salt and freshly ground black pepper

Pull the leaves off the rosemary stalks, leaving just the tufts at the end. Sharpen the other end to a point. Thread the monkfish and prawns onto the rosemary stalks and season with salt and pepper. Put to one side.

For the dressing, cut the peppers, chilli and black olives, and chop the chives. Add 100ml of the olive oil and a dash of lemon juice.

Cook the pasta in plenty of boiling water. Drain, then mix the pasta with the remaining 25ml of olive oil, tomato concasse, and salt and pepper.

Pan-fry the monkfish and prawns for about 2 minutes on each side. Squeeze a wedge of lemon over and leave to rest.

Put the pasta into bowls, add the dressing, put the monkfish and prawns on top and serve.

BAKED PANATTONE PUDDING
WITH ESPRESSO CREME ANGLAISE

For the Panattone:

25g fresh yeast

140ml warm water + 5 Tbsp extra

250g castor sugar + 2 Tbsp extra

24 egg yolks

300g melted butter

1 tsp Salt

1kg plain flour

Sultanas soaked in Amaretto

20ml Amaretto

For the pudding mix:

14 eggs

1 Ltr milk

1 Ltr cream

500g sugar

A splash of Amaretto

2 vanilla pods

Zest of 1 lemon

Brown sugar

For the crème anglaise:

8 egg yolks

75g sugar

300ml milk

300ml double cream

1 vanilla pod

300ml espresso,
  reduced to 150ml

20ml Amaretto

For the panattone, dissolve the yeast in 5 Tbsp of warm water with 2 Tbsp of sugar. Place the yeast mixture, the egg yolks, butter, salt and 500g of flour into a large bowl and beat until they form a paste.

Add the rest of the flour, water, sugar, the sultanas and Amaretto, and work until a ball forms. Put the mix in a warm place and leave to prove until the size has doubled. This process takes several hours.

Punch down the dough and place onto a baking tray. Allow the mix to prove again. Bake in a hot oven (180°C, Gas Mark 5) until the top is dark brown.

For the pudding mix, crack the eggs into a bowl. Place the cream, milk, lemon zest, Amaretto and vanilla pods in a pot, and bring to the boil. Mix together the eggs and sugar. Then whisk in the hot cream.

Slice the panattone, and arrange in a deep roasting tray. Pour over the cream mixture and cover with brown sugar. Bake in a bain marie until golden and moist.

For the crème anglaise, whisk together the egg yolks and sugar. Heat together the cream, milk, espresso, vanilla and Amaretto. Pour into the egg yolks, then return to a low heat. Thicken the anglaise, stirring constantly, until the mixture coats the back of a wooden spoon.

DEREK MARSHALL

'To be a great chef is to achieve consistency— to guarantee that a dish will taste at least as good as it did last time'

At school, I wasn't very interested in academic subjects so I was sent along to the careers office. Fortunately, they discovered something I hadn't recognised until then—my interest in cooking—and I started on a training scheme at The Fountain Restaurant. I seemed to have a knack for cooking, so I put everything into that job, and it turned out to be a great training ground and the start of my career.

I also owe a lot to Jim Kerr at Rogano. His guiding principle, which I have tried to follow, is to keep things simple—and it always works. If it becomes complicated, then you will probably get out of your depth. After keeping things simple, the key to becoming a great chef is consistency—to be able to guarantee that a dish will taste at least as good as it did last time, each and every time it is served.

When I read a menu, I like to know exactly what's in the recipe with no hidden extras. What you read is what you get. So the food I like to cook is very basic, with nothing too exotic or out of place. I have found that Glasgow people, especially, like a good, filling dinner, but at the same time they are becoming more aware of the pitfalls of unhealthy eating. I think one of the reasons why Gamba is such a success is that we are aware of this aspect of modern eating, an awareness that is reflected in the emphasis we place on fresh and affordable fish dishes.

Fish has certainly become much more popular in recent times, owing to a diminishing interest in meat and an increasing emphasis on health and fitness in general. This delights me, as fish is good to work with—it's clean and healthy, and looks great on a plate.

And so to the recipies. A good fish restaurant wouldn't be right if the fish soup wasn't and I'm sure you will enjoy this one. Halibut is a tasty, meaty fish which is delicious with mussels and saffron. Finally, after all that healthy eating there's no better way to end a meal than with a truly sinful pudding.

FISH SOUP
WITH CRAB MEAT, STEM GINGER AND CORIANDER

275g white fish meat (haddock, cod or whiting)

4 cloves of garlic

50g root ginger

2 medium onions, chopped

50g unsalted butter

3 Tbsp plain flour

1.15 Ltr fish stock

1 packet of coriander

50g grated stem ginger

3 Tbsp tomato purée

450g white crab meat

75ml brandy

Melt the butter over a low heat in a thick-bottomed pan.

Chop the onions, garlic and root ginger, and sweat in a covered pan with the butter. Add brandy and reduce.

Mix in the flour and cook out for about five minutes, still on a low heat. Add the tomato purée and keep mixing. Start adding fish stock little by little, mixing all the time.

Add the white fish meat and cook for 30 to 40 minutes.

Liquidise the soup, and pass through a sieve into a clean pot or bowl. Add the crab meat, grated stem ginger and chopped coriander.

Serve in warm soup bowls with garlic bread.

SEARED HALIBUT

WITH BABY ONION AND SAFFRON STEW

4 halibut fillets (about 150-175g each)

24 small onions (the smaller the better)

1 clove of garlic

20g butter

10g saffron strands

2 Tbsp chives

200ml white wine

200ml fish stock

200ml double cream

200g mussel meat

Slowly melt the butter in a pan, add the baby onions and garlic, and sweat until the onions colour slightly, then remove them.

Add the white wine to the pan and reduce by half, then add the fish stock and simmer. Add the double cream and reduce further.

Place a frying pan on quite a high heat with a little vegetable oil. When it starts to smoke, add the halibut, presentation side first, and reduce the heat. When slightly brown, remove from the pan and place on the bottom half of the grill.

Add the mussel meat to the cream sauce, along with the saffron and onions.

Take the mussels and onions out of the sauce with a perforated spoon, and place them in the centre of a flat pasta plate. Place the halibut on top.

Add chives to the sauce, pour a little on to the plate and serve.

BANANA, COCONUT AND MAPLE SYRUP CHEESECAKE

400g ginger nut biscuits

100g unsalted butter

1kg Philadelphia cheese

200g white chocolate

500ml double cream

30g toasted dessicated coconut

150ml maple syrup

2 bananas (one chopped for cheesecake,

  one sliced for caramelising)

Sprig of fresh mint

Melt the butter over a low heat. Place the ginger nuts in a food processor, add to the butter and press into the base of a cheesecake tin. Chill for 30 minutes.

Whisk the double cream until it reaches the ribbon stage, and chill.

Place the Philadelphia in a mixing bowl and beat until soft. Add the chopped banana, melted chocolate, maple syrup and coconut. When mixed together, fold in the double cream, pour into the cheesecake tin and refrigerate overnight.

Unclip the tin and shake it a little until the cheesecake comes away from the edges.

With a warm knife, portion the cake into ten pieces, always starting with an equal half-moon shape.

Take three slices of the second banana and dust with icing sugar, blow torch (or grill) and leave to cool.

Dribble some maple syrup on to the bottom of each plate and place a slice of cheese-cake on top. Arrange the caramelised bananas on top and garnish with fresh mint.

JAMES MURPHY

'A kitchen team is like a football team, it needs a good manager, good players, time and effort'

A kitchen team is like a football team, it needs a good manager, good players, time and effort. I'm one of those people who is hungry for work and needs to be busy constantly, and I have always enjoyed working as a hotel chef—hotel life holds my interest and gives me a 'buzz'. It's a career that's given me the opportunity to work with some great chefs—like Anton Mossiman at The Dorchester Hotel in London. He is a genius in the kitchen and I have never stopped feeling admiration for his work. I'm still learning every day and I try to lead by example by being hands-on and enthusiastic.

Hotel chefs must be adaptable and spontaneous, but there are always occasions which strike you dumb, even if only for a second. I remember making watercress soup for a function of 100 at the Royal Crescent Hotel in Bath. All that was left to do was to liquidise the soup, but the unfortunate commis chef chosen for the job got a bit carried away and managed to spray the entire potful around the kitchen. When I got over the initial shock of seeing the green sludge covering practically every surface, my first reaction was to cool down the young chef who had been covered in boiling green mush. So, with some help he was dropped into a large sink full of cold water. I was then left to prepare another pot of watercress soup—having used all the watercress already, I took every piece of green veg I could find, boiled the whole lot up and made an instant 'watercress' soup. As the soup was served, the boy was still sitting in the sink with his socks and shoes floating around him.

My aim is to continue to improve the food outlets at The Glasgow Moat House. When catering for vast numbers of people, speed is of the essence, but at the same time there must be no compromising of flavours and presentation.

CONFIT OF OAK SMOKED SOLE
WITH WARM POTATOES AND SPRING ONIONS

2 whole sole

Chinese five spice

250g duck fat

2 spring onions, cut on the slant

4 baking potatoes

250g butter

4 Tbsp vinaigrette

1 tomato, cut into concasse

4 piece solferino (small scoops) of carrot, cucumber and courgette

Roll the sole fillets into paupiettes and skewer with cocktail sticks. Dust the fish with Chinese five spice and sear.

Poach in duck fat for 2-3 minutes, then finish in the oven at 220°C (Gas Mark 7) for approximately 5 minutes, frequently checking to see if they are cooked.

Peel the 4 baking potatoes and cut into cylindrical shapes with a round cutter. Cook in butter until the butter has clarified and has given a golden brown potato fondant.

Make the vinaigrette using three parts oil to one part balsamic or sherry vinegar.

To serve, place the potato fondant on a plate, slice the sole and place on top. Sprinkle with tomato in concasse and chopped spring onions. Finish with drizzles of vinaigrette and solferino of vegetables.

THE MODERNISED 'BIG BREAKFAST'

240g Stornoway black pudding

220g pork fillet

12 quails' eggs

100g wild mushrooms

8 cherry tomatoes

30g haricot beans

Chicken stock

240g potatoes

70g smoked bacon in lardons

Grill the black pudding and char-grill the pork fillet and cherry tomatoes.

Cut and sauté the potatoes and poach the quails' eggs.

Meanwhile fry the bacon lardons and mushrooms, and cook the haricot beans in chicken stock.

Present with the pork fillet on top of the potatoes in the centre of the plate. Place 3 quenelles of black pudding, 3 poached quails' eggs and a couple of cherry tomatoes around the outside. Scatter the plate with wild mushrooms, lardons and haricot beans.

BONED QUAIL AND PIGEON FORESTIERE STYLE

4 whole boneless quail

2 whole squab pigeon

4 slices Parma ham

12 large new potatoes

12 baby onions

$1/4$ savoy cabbage

1 shallot

Pinch of caraway

2 Ltr veal stock

2 Ltr game stock

25g mirepoix (carrot, onion,
  leek and celery roughly chopped,
  boiled and strained out)

Sprig of thyme

Sprig of tarragon

500ml malt whisky

300ml port

25g butter

Seasoning

For the Mousseline:

200g chicken breast

$1^1/_2$ egg whites

550ml double cream

Seasoning

Bone the pigeon, remove breasts and seal in a hot pan and allow to cool.

To make the mousseline, blitz the egg whites and chicken breasts with a blender until a 'rubbery' consistency is achieved. Add the cream slowly to prevent the mixture from splitting. Season.

Wrap the cooled pigeon breasts in the Parma ham, savoy cabbage and a little mousseline.

Open out the quail, skin-side down on top of some tin foil, spread a little mousseline inside and place the pigeon in the centre.

Fold the quail back into shape using the tin foil, and sear and roast in a pan until pink.

Turn and roast the potatoes, and sauté the cabbage with caraway. Simmer the onions in a little stock and then colour in a pan.

Sear the pigeon bones in a pan with the mirepoix, add the alcohol and the rest of the stock and reduce to make the sauce. Finally, infuse with herbs. To serve, place the cabbage in the centre of each plate, place the pigeon on top with a garnish and spoon the sauce around the outside.

PEAR CLAFOUTIS
WITH MACERATED PRUNES, PRUNE NUTS
AND LEMON-FLAVOURED YOGHURT ICE-CREAM

For the sweet paste:

255g plain flour

25g ground almonds

1 egg

125g butter

85g icing sugar

Water

4 drops lemon juice

$1/2$ vanilla pod

For the pastry cream:

400ml milk

50g sugar

2 egg yolks

25g plain flour

$1/4$ lemon zest

1 vanilla pod

For soaking the prunes:

150g dried prunes

300ml stock syrup

Zest of 2 oranges and lemons

$1/4$ cinnamon stick

Measure of Armagnac

Star anise

2 pears

Clafoutis mix:

2 eggs

25g sugar

A few drops of lemon juice

For the ice cream:

6 leaves lemon balm

200ml white wine

200g sugar

100ml lemon juice

150g yoghurt

300g whipped cream

Place the prunes in stock syrup with the zest of lemon and orange, the cinnamon stick, star anise and Armagnac and cook gently until tender and plump. Cool in stock and leave to infuse for up to 2 weeks.

To prepare the sweet paste, cream the butter and sugar together until light and fluffy. Add the egg slowly until well incorporated, then add the sifted flour and ground almonds. Add the lemon juice, vanilla seeds and a touch of water, and mix well until the paste is of the correct consistency, then rest for two hours.

To form the tartlets, roll the paste until rather thin, line tartlet cases with the paste and bake the tartlets blind until just cooked. Refrigerate until required.

For the pastry cream, bring the milk to the boil with the vanilla pod and lemon zest, and simmer gently. Pour on to the egg yolks and sugar, keeping back some of the milk. Mix this remaining milk with the flour and add to the pastry cream. Cook until the cream has thickened and the flour is cooked out. Remove the vanilla pod last of all and allow to cool. Top with a butter paper.

For the clafoutis, mix the pastry cream with the egg yolks. Whisk the egg whites to a peak, add sugar and lemon juice, and incorporate. Add the pastry cream to the egg whites by gently folding in.

Stone the prunes, and skin and dice the pears. Place into the tartlets. Pour clafoutis batter into the tartlets and bake in the oven at 180°C (Gas mark 4) for 10 minutes, then remove from the oven and serve.

For the ice cream, marinade a small bunch of lemon balm in white wine for two hours. Pass on to sugar and boil. Cool, then add lemon juice and yoghurt. Add whipped cream and freeze.

NICK NAIRN

'As I travelled the length and breadth of Scotland, getting involved with the raw ingredients of my trade, I began to learn the value of using the best produce, properly sourced and freshly cooked'

It was only out of necessity that I learned to cook. At 25 I was a navigating officer in the Merchant Navy, and when I went on study leave, I was suddenly faced with the prospect of having to cook for myself, as I didn't have enough money to eat out. I couldn't boil an egg, but I had to start somewhere, so I bought a frying pan, a wooden spoon, and a copy of *Country House Cooking* by Elizabeth Kent. This excellent book (now unfortunately out of print) introduced me to the complexities of restaurant food. I never looked back, becoming so fascinated with cooking fairly complicated dishes at home that I soon started hosting my own dinner parties.

After leaving the Merchant Navy, I decided to open my own restaurant, and so set about restoring Braeval Old Mill, which opened in 1986. The place was wildly successful, but made hardly any money. On the other hand, it did wonders for my confidence—a string of awards came my way, most notably a Michelin 'Red M' in 1990, and a Michelin Star in 1991. This was a turning point—I had found something I could do, and do very well. But it was only the beginning.

In 1995 I started doing television, and this completely changed my life. The *Wild Harvest* and *Island Harvest* series took me out of the restaurant, and brought me into contact with a wide variety of people who actually caught or grew the food I cooked. As I travelled the length and breadth of Scotland, getting involved with the raw ingredients of my trade, I began to learn the value of using the best produce, properly sourced and freshly cooked. Not only that, but I realised that the most important thing is to keep it simple—if the essential ingredients are right, there is no need for elaboration.

This is the philosophy behind Nairn's, which my brother and I opened in 1997. Housed in an elegant Georgian townhouse, Nairn's is glamorous and modern, with the feel of a London restaurant, while the food is classical with a modern twist, and the atmosphere is restful. We are extremely busy, but it is frustrating that, as the manager, I don't get to spend as much time in the kitchen as I would like.

What does bring me great pleasure is to see the emergence of a new generation of restaurateurs joining ranks with the long-established stalwarts. Together they are elevating Scottish cooking to a level where it will shrug off the shackles of the haggis and the deep-fried Mars bar, and Scotland will be well and truly placed on the culinary map.

SQUASH SOUP
WITH TOMATO AND PARMESAN

2 butternut squash

4 Tbsp olive oil

2 plum tomatoes

30g grated Parmesan

2 large potatoes, peeled and sliced

1 onion, sliced

120g butter

2 Tbsp chopped chives to garnish

900ml vegetable nage or water

Maldon salt

Freshly ground white pepper

Peel the butternut squash, split lengthways, remove the seeds and roughly chop, toss in the olive oil and roast in the oven for 20 minutes.

In a large saucepan, sweat the onion in the butter, add the potato and sweat for a further 10 minutes without colouring. Add the squash and vegetable nage, and cook for a further 10-15 minutes then remove from heat.

Take the tomatoes and blanche for 10 seconds, peel, cut in half and deseed. Take the soup and blend in a food processor, strain through a sieve, then adjust the seasoning to taste and keep warm. Ladle the soup into large bowls, place half a tomato in the centre of each, and sprinkle with Parmesan and freshly chopped chives.

BRAISED SHIN OF ANGUS BEEF
WITH PARSNIP MASHED POTATO AND SHALLOT GRAVY

750g trimmed beef shin, cut into cubes

450g spinach

5 Tbsp olive oil

1 onion, finely chopped

3 carrots, cut into small dice

4 cloves garlic, finely chopped

2 sprigs thyme

2 sprigs rosemary

550ml red wine

550ml chicken stock

3 parsnips, peeled and roughly chopped

4 large floury potatoes (e.g. King Edward),
  peeled and roughly chopped

100g unsalted butter

20 small shallots, peeled

60ml cream

1 Tbsp fresh chopped tarragon

Maldon salt & Freshly ground white pepper

Preheat the oven to 160°C (Gas mark 3). Season the beef shin well with salt and pepper, then heat a large frying pan to very hot, add 1 Tbsp olive oil and add the beef in batches. Sear each piece for 4-5 minutes on each side to colour and seal it.

In a large oven-proof casserole on the hob, melt 25g of the butter and gently cook the onion, carrots and garlic until they become translucent. Add the herbs and seared beef shin and cook for another 5 minutes. Add the red wine and chicken stock and bring to the boil. Then carefully transfer to the oven and cook for 2 hours. Meanwhile, make the mash by filling a large pan with water to cover the potatoes and the parsnips, and bringing it to the boil. Season the water well with a large pinch of salt. Simmer for 20 minutes or until tender. Drain very well and then mash or pass through a Mouli. Finish by adding the cream and rest of the butter—beating it in well. Keep warm by putting an old butter wrapper over it still in the pan—set over a very low heat.

Take the shallots and roast off in a hot pan with 3 Tbsp of olive oil. When they have started to caramelise and give off their own juices put in the oven with the beef for 10-15 minutes until they are sticky and tender. Remove the casserole from the oven and separate the beef and the sauce. Strain the sauce into a pan and simmer until it has reduced by half. Add the shallots and keep the sauce warm. Pick the spinach and wash it, heat a large pan to very hot and add the last tablespoon of olive oil—sauté the spinach until it has just started to wilt and become soft.

Shred the beef—it should be so tender that it pulls apart easily—and add a little of the reduced sauce to bind it. Heat the beef and reheat the mash. To serve, place a spoonful of mash in the centre of each warmed plate. Place a portion of spinach on top and then place the beef on top of that. Spoon the sauce and shallots around. Garnish with some freshly chopped tarragon.

STEAMED ROULADE OF SKATE

WITH TAPENADE & RATATOUILLE BROTH

1 Tbsp olive oil

4 large skate wings, trimmed and skinned

2 courgettes, cut into 5mm dice

For the tapenade:

2 cloves of garlic, finely chopped

100g anchovy fillets

100g salted capers, rinsed and drained

100g pitted olives

3 Tbsp virgin olive oil

Squeeze of lemon juice

For the ratatouille:

1 courgette

2 red peppers, roasted and skinned

1 sprig of thyme

1 yellow pepper, roasted and skinned

1 aubergine,

2 plum tomatoes, skinned

600ml nage or vegetable stock

Maldon salt

Freshly ground white pepper

Chervil

First make the tapenade by combining everything except the olive oil in a food processor. Blitz until the mix forms a coarse paste. Then add the olive oil and mix again. Set aside until needed.

To make the ratatouille, cut all the vegetables into 5mm dice. Add one of the red peppers and the thyme to the nage, and simmer for 20 minutes. Blitz the pepper, thyme and stock with a hand blender thoroughly, then leave to strain through a fine muslin cloth, retaining the juice in a jug.

Put the pepper juice in a pan and add the diced vegetables, check the seasoning, then set aside.

In a large heavy-based frying pan heat the olive oil to hot. Season the skate wings with salt and pepper and then cook in the pan until sealed (1 minute each side). You will probably have to cook the wings in batches. Leave the skate to cool, then remove the meat from the bones.

Lay a large piece of cling-film (about 30cm square) on a work surface, and lay the fish meat out over the cling-film. With a palette knife spread a thin layer of tapenade evenly across the fish.

Using the cling-film, roll the fish as tightly and evenly as you can away from you—in the same way that you would do for a Swiss roll. Once rolled, tie the cling film at each end, roll the whole thing in a fresh layer of cling film and then refrigerate for at least four hours.

With a sharp knife cut the roulade into four 7cm slices and place them in a steamer for 3-4 minutes. Heat the ratatouille through.

Remove the skate from the steamer and place each piece in the center of a large warmed bowl. Spoon around the ratatouille broth and garnish with some sprigs of chervil.

CHIVAS PARFAIT

WITH PRUNES AND EARL GREY SYRUP

5 egg yolks

300ml double cream

75ml Chivas Regal whisky

75g castor sugar, dissolved in 3 Tbsp of water

1 Tbsp lemon juice

For the Earl Grey prunes:

300ml water

300g castor sugar

1 Tbsp Earl Grey tea leaves

16 Agen prunes

To make the Earl Grey syrup, dissolve the sugar in the water in a large pan, and boil for five minutes—allowing the syrup to reduce a little. Add the tea leaves and allow to infuse for 6 minutes. Pass the syrup through a sieve and add the prunes to the still-hot liquid. Season with lemon juice and 25ml of the Chivas. Place in a tub and allow to cool, then store in the fridge. The prunes can be used straight away but the flavour improves the longer you leave them.

To make the parfait, whisk the egg yolks in an electric mixer until they are very pale and well risen in volume. Whip the cream with the rest of the whisky until it just starts to thicken.

Boil the castor sugar and three tablespoons of water until it reaches the softball stage (i.e. dip in a cold teaspoon, coating it, then dip this into cold water to set, and pinch a little between finger and thumb—when it can be rolled into a soft ball it is ready).

With the mixer running on full speed, slowly pour the softball sugar onto the yolks. Reduce the speed by half and whisk for a further 5 minutes.

Fold together the yolk and syrup mix and the whipped cream, pour into a freezer-proof container or 12 x 125ml dariole moulds and freeze immediately.

To serve, reheat the syrup and prunes gently. Serve each guest 3 scoops of parfait or 1 turned out dariole mould, then arrange four warmed prunes around the scoops and drizzle the Earl Grey syrup artistically around.

PHILIP RASKIN

'When I'm told "it can't be done" I usually respond that man has successfully landed on and returned from the moon and that, in comparison, my request is relatively uncomplicated'

We embarked on this enterprise with neither training nor experience; a course of action not to be recommended and, as we discovered, laced with danger.

There is, however, one significant advantage—a totally fresh approach. To borrow a phrase, we adopted and adapted—which is another way of saying we made it up as we went along. A generous dollop of blissful ignorance and being a particularly stubborn Taurean also helps.

It's fair to say that at The Inn on the Green we're unashamedly quirky. We seldom purchase 'off-the-shelf' items, and often want suppliers to adapt their products to our needs.

When I'm told "it can't be done" I usually respond that man has successfully landed on and returned from the moon and that, in comparison, my request is relatively uncomplicated.

The Inn on the Green is all about people as well as product—the fare is important, naturally—but it's not everything.

The front of house staff are long-served and friendly and our equally long-served chefs take great pride in their work. The menu is extensive, the portions ample and the quality first class.

Nevertheless, I've learnt that you can't be all things to all people—you can't please all of the people all of the time and you must recognise your own limitations. When you're unsure, say "can't do". You won't lose a customer, you'll probably gain one. Customers will forgive the odd mistake, but will not tolerate aggression, unfriendliness or being treated as invisible. If we spill wine down your shirt, we'll do it with a smile.

Although the restaurant is frequently refurbished, we have hardly changed the decor since day one—green hessian walls, peach ceiling and a scruffy wooden floor. The only change guests remark upon is me—older, bespectacled and a lot fuller about the face!

The restaurant is like one of our children. With a parent's sixth sense, I know when all is not well. I hear the noises and see the signs only a parent recognises. I'm very particular about the company our child keeps and naturally I worry endlessly when I'm parted from baby. As this book goes to press, we're completing our conversion into an eighteen bedroom hotel. We have neither training nor experience—here we go again!

SALMON WRAPPED IN SAVOY CABBAGE
ON A BED OF SMOKED SALMON MOUSSELINE
WITH A SAFFRON AND GINGER SAUCE

4 x 220g salmon fillets

1 medium-sized savoy cabbage

For the Mousseline:

1 egg white

450g smoked salmon

50ml double cream

Large pinch of dill

Large pinch of chives

Seasoning

For the Saffron and Ginger Sauce:

25g butter

1 small onion, finely chopped

75ml chicken stock

1 Tbsp grated ginger

75ml white wine

150ml double cream

2 Tbsp chopped parsley

2 Tbsp chopped chives

1 clove of garlic

1 pinch of saffron (in a little water)

To make the mousseline, place the smoked salmon in a blender for one minute, add the egg white and mix for another minute. Slowly add in the double cream, then the herbs, and season to taste. Place the mousseline into shallow, round moulds and cool in the fridge for an hour.

Meanwhile, prepare the saffron and ginger sauce. Melt the butter in a saucepan. Add the onion, grated ginger and garlic. Add the white wine and chicken stock, and reduce by half. Add the cream to the liquid mixture and simmer for about 10 minutes. Add the saffron in water, chives and parsley, and reduce the sauce further to a nice glaze. Season to taste.

Remove the hard stalk from the cabbage and plunge the leaves into boiling water for 20 seconds. Remove quickly and put straight into cold water.

Lay the cabbage leaves out flat, and place the salmon fillets on top. Wrap the cabbage around tightly. Season and steam the salmon for 7 to 10 minutes, depending on the thickness of the fillets.

Warm the mousseline by steaming for 3 to 5 minutes.

To serve, spoon the sauce onto a plate. Take the mousseline from the moulds and lay the salmon fillets on top.

WHISKY AND LIME MARINATED SALMON

900g of side of salmon, finely sliced

1 measure of whisky

1 lime

150ml olive oil

50ml white wine vinegar

25g dill

25g coriander

Seasoning and dressing as required

Lay the sliced salmon on a 3cm deep tray.

In a bowl, mix the olive oil and zest of lime. Place the dill, coriander, whisky, lime juice and vinegar in a blender and mix for 1 minute. Slowly add the oil mixture and blend for 2 more minutes. Lightly season to taste.

Pour the marinade over the salmon, and refrigerate for at least 6 hours.

Once the salmon has marinated, place under the grill for 2 minutes.

To serve, place the salmon on a bed of green salad, pour on your preferred dressing and serve.

PAN-FRIED DUCK

WITH A PLUM, PORT AND CINNAMON SAUCE
ON A BED OF STIR-FRIED JULIENNE VEGETABLES

4 x 225g duck breasts

1 Tbsp of oil

50g carrots

50g leeks

50g peppers

Honey

For the sauce:

150ml of duck or game stock

1 Tbsp of oil

2 Tbsp of plain flour

50g castor sugar

50ml red wine vinegar

225g plums

Pinch of cinnamon

1 measure of port

30g carrots

30g onions

For the sauce: Heat the oil in a saucepan, add the onion and carrot, and cook until lightly browned.

Add the flour, then stir and cook gently until browned a little. Add the hot stock, bring to the boil, cover and simmer for 30 minutes.

In another saucepan, melt the sugar over a low heat and cook until it begins to turn a light golden colour. Add the vinegar slowly, and keep stirring until the sugar is dissolved in the vinegar. Then add cinnamon to taste.

Strain the sauce made from the stock into a measuring jug, pour carefully on to the sugar mixture and cook gently for 10 minutes. Add the stoned, halved plums and cook for 5 minutes to warm through, then add the port.

Place the mixture in the liquidiser and strain. Add seasoning as required.

To cook the duck, heat a frying pan with oil, place the breasts in the pan and gently fry for 5 minutes, turning once.

Brush the duck with melted honey, and then place in the oven at 220°C (Gas mark 7) for about 15 minutes. Allow to cool a little and then slice the breasts.

Slice the leeks, and julienne the carrots and peppers. Fry lightly in a little oil.

To serve, spoon some of the mixed vegetables onto the centre of each plate, put a duck breast on top and spoon some sauce around.

COURGETTE AND SWEET POTATO STRUDEL

2 rectangles of filo pastry (approx. 20cm x 40cm)

450g courgettes

450g sweet potatoes

$1/2$ tsp cinnamon

1 tsp garlic

50g butter

25g freshly chopped coriander

1 medium-sized onion

$1/2$ tsp mixed spices

1 egg

Dice the sweet potatoes and fry gently for 7 to 10 minutes until al dente. Dice the onion, add to the potatoes, and fry for one minute. Add the garlic, cinnamon, mixed spices, coriander and diced courgette, and fry for a further 2 minutes. Season to taste and allow to cool.

Lay out the sheets of filo pastry, brush the rim of the pastry with melted butter and place the cooled potato and courgette mixture on top of the pastry. Form into a Swiss roll. Brush with egg wash (whisked egg) and bake at Gas mark 4 (180°C) for 15 minutes.

Remove from the oven and serve on a bed of dressed salad.

FERRIER RICHARDSON

'I don't expect people to pay homage to a plate—they should be able to loosen their ties, relax and enjoy the whole experience'

I don't expect people to pay homage to a plate—they should be able to loosen their ties a little, relax and enjoy the whole experience. It's easy for attention to detail to get lost, but the personal approach in a restaurant is really important to me. Ambience and service play a big part in the whole experience of eating out—I've always believed that you need to be in the right frame of mind to enjoy a meal.

Food is an ever-changing and fashionable market, and it's important to keep ahead of the game, to keep developing new ideas—so I am always on the hunt for something new. Foreign travel has become one of the greatest influences on food—people can now get to previously inaccessible places, and having sampled the local fare they no longer accept poor imitations when they return. For me, visiting new places and experiencing different cultures is very important. I've incorporated many influences into my work, but the Far East—where fantastic fresh produce is combined with a complex palate of flavours—has been a particularly rich source of inspiration.

Sometimes, however, there's no getting away from the Scottish climate. At a glamorous corporate function at October Cafe, a light drizzle started overhead during the first course, and quickly turned into a downpour—thanks to a faulty sprinkler system. Despite the soaking, all 250 guests moved downstairs and carried on with the party. Far from being a washout, it turned out to be one of the best nights we had there. They even booked ahead for Christmas—when one guest turned up in a frogman's outfit carrying a huge umbrella, just in case.

I have always been ambitious and my next goal is to open a restaurant in New York. The Americans are such open and positive people—and, as the song says, if you can make it there, you can make it anywhere.

GATEAU OF SMOKED SALMON
WITH A DILL DRESSING

240g finely diced smoked salmon

60g crushed oatcakes

4 tsp clarified butter

4 tsp finely chopped dill

4 tsp finely chopped red pepper

4 tsp finely chopped onion

4 tsp small capers

120g cream cheese

Mix the crushed oatcakes with clarified butter and line the bottom of four 6cm rings. Next, mix the salmon, dill, pepper, onion and capers and fill the prepared moulds, leaving a 5mm gap at the top. Spread the cream cheese on top.

For the dill dressing:

24 slices channelled cucumber

4 tsp keta

4 sprigs of chervil

16 cubes of potato, poached in saffron

4 Tbsp dill oil

Seasoning

8 cherry tomatoes, halved

Place the cucumber slices in a circle in the centre of each plate. Place a gateau in the centre of the cucumber, and remove the ring. Top with keta and a sprig of chervil. Alternate the potatoes and cherry tomatoes. Garnish with dill oil.

SEARED TERIYAKI SALMON WITH GINGER VEGETABLES

AND AN OYSTER SAUCE

4 x 175g salmon fillets

120ml teriyaki sauce

50g red peppers, shaped into squares

50g yellow peppers, shaped into squares

8 asparagus spears, trimmed

4 baby courgettes

8 spring onions, trimmed

25g fresh ginger

8 small chillies

8 water chestnuts, halved

25ml sesame oil

120ml oyster sauce

Marinate the salmon fillets in the teriyaki sauce for one hour.

Clean, trim and shape all the vegetables and spices. Prepare the grill or griddle pan and cook the vegetables with a light glaze of sesame oil.

Sear the salmon in a very hot non-stick or cast iron frying pan with a little sesame oil. Two minutes on either side will keep the salmon pink.

Pipe the oyster sauce on a plate, garnish with the vegetables and place the salmon on top.

ROAST TURBOT

WITH PROVENCAL VEGETABLES,
FETTA CHEESE AND A BASIL DRESSING

4 x 175g fillets of turbot

4 x 8cm diameter, 5mm thick, discs of fetta cheese

1 large courgette

1 medium aubergine

4 plum tomatoes

16 spring onions

1 red pepper

1 yellow pepper

1 packet basil leaves (supermarket size)

$1/2$ packet Italian parsley

200ml olive oil

Seasoning

Channel the courgette and slice diagonally 1cm thick. Slice the aubergine into 1cm thick circles. Clean and trim the spring onions into 15cm lengths. Halve the plum tomatoes lengthwise. Cut the peppers into 1cm squares. Char-grill or mark the vegetables on a griddle pan, season, drizzle with olive oil and place in an oven to finish.

Seal the turbot in a hot heavy pan, place in the oven and roast at 220°C (Gas mark 7) for 4 minutes.

Blanch the basil and parsley, refresh and squeeze dry. Blend with the oil and season.

To serve, make a gateau with two slices of aubergine per slice of fetta cheese. Warm in the oven. Place the gateau in the centre of a plate, surround with the courgette, tomato, peppers and spring onions. Top the gateau with the turbot. Drizzle with the olive oil and basil dressing.

WHISKY AND SHORTBREAD TRUFFLES

625g plain chocolate

150ml double cream

300g butter, at room temperature

50ml malt whisky

125g shortbread (Walkers, crushed into small rib size)

500g cocoa powder

Chop up the chocolate, and melt in a bain marie.

Bring the cream to the boil, then allow to cool. Add to the chocolate.

Beat the butter until it is light. Incorporate the cool chocolate mixture a little at a time. Add the whisky and broken shortbread.

Mould into chocolate size balls, roll in cocoa powder and refrigerate for one hour before serving.

WILLIAM SIMPSON

'Rogano has always stood for the unsurpassed luxury and perfect elegance of the finest fish and seafood'

In 1935, as the great Cunard liner *Queen Mary* took shape on the Clyde, a restaurant was refitted in the same Art Deco style—and a Glasgow legend was born.

With its unique 1930s ambience, Rogano is the oldest surviving restaurant in Glasgow. For sixty years its chefs have dedicated themselves to the delicate art of cooking and serving the finest fish and seafood in the world—fish and seafood from Scottish waters—and I am extremely proud to be a part of that tradition.

Lunch at Rogano is a Glasgow institution. But for all its traditions, its inimitable style, and its loyal clientele, Rogano is a friendly place, with a special welcome for the traveller—it is, of course, perfectly situated for the city's most elegant shops and many of its leading cultural venues.

As the hour advances, the mood changes. The city suits disperse, the young and fashionable assemble in the bar, and Glasgow's lovers of fine food and wine gather to dine, as they have done for sixty years.

Whilst food fashions have come and gone, Rogano has always stood for the unsurpassed luxury and perfect elegance of the finest fish and seafood—salmon, langoustines, scallops, lobster, halibut and oysters—faultlessly prepared and presented in classic style.

This selection of some of my favourite recipes from the restaurant should provide an insight into why it has retained its place among the very best in the city.

SEARED SALMON
ON A RADICCHIO PESTO

4 x 250g salmon fillets,
 with skin left on
Olive oil for frying
Parsley and thyme for garnish

For the pesto:
1 head of radicchio
100g cooked beetroot
100g pine nuts
100g grated Parmesan
2 cloves garlic
75ml good quality olive oil

Sear the salmon, skin side down, in a little oil on a moderate heat for 1 minute to crisp the skin.

Turn the salmon carefully, making sure that the skin stays on. Cook on a low heat for a further 5 minutes or until cooked. Keep warm.

For the pesto, blend all the ingredients together in a food processor, adding the oil last. Season to taste.

To serve, gently heat the pesto until it is warmed through, then put some in the centre of each plate. Warm the salmon under the grill, and place on top of the pesto. Garnish with herbs.

GRILLED LANGOUSTINES
WITH GARLIC AND HERB BUTTER

24 whole fresh langoustines

3 lemons

Fresh herbs (dill, parsley, chervil)

2 cloves garlic

300g butter

Split each langoustine down its back with a chopping knife, starting just behind the head joint. Cut right through to the bottom of the tail and pull open. Place on a grilling tray.

Melt the butter, and chop the herbs and garlic finely or blend in a food processor. Add the butter and the juice of one lemon. Spoon the butter mixture over the open langoustine tails, then cook under a low to medium grill. This will take only a few minutes. Finish off under a high grill.

Cut the remaining two lemons in half, and garnish with sprigs of herbs.

To serve, place six langoustines on each plate, three on the bottom, then two, then one, giving the dish height. Spoon butter from the grilling tray over the tails, and place a lemon half on the side.

FEUILLETTE
OF SEARED SCALLOPS

WITH SQUID INK SAUCE
AND SPRING ONIONS

20 good-sized king scallops

2 bunches of spring onions, chopped

4 sheets of filo pastry

50g chopped herbs (parsley, dill, basil)

A little egg wash

For the sauce:

300ml good quality fish stock

2 sachets of squid ink

1 measure Noilly Prat (or similar dry vermouth)

25g plain flour

25g unsalted butter

Seasoning

To make the feuillette, cut 24 10cm triangles of filo. Egg wash these, and sprinkle herbs over them. Place one triangle on top of another to give 8 triangular pieces, each one three layers high. Cook these on a buttered tray in a moderate oven until golden brown.

For the sauce, make a roux with the flour and butter. Stir in the fish stock until you have a smooth fish velouté that coats the back of a wooden spoon. Add the Noilly Prat and squid ink, and season to taste. Keep warm.

To serve, pan sear the scallops on both sides, and place in the oven for 2-3 minutes. Blanch the chopped spring onions for one minute in hot water.

Sauce each plate and put three scallops on the sauce. Place a piece of filo on the three scallops, then add two more scallops on top, followed by another piece of filo on top of this. Garnish by sprinkling the spring onions around.

BAKED MONKFISH STEAK
WITH ROAST CAPSICUM AND BALSAMIC DRESSING

1 small red pepper

1 small green pepper

1 small yellow pepper

2 lemons

4 x 250g monkfish steaks

50ml balsamic vinegar

200ml olive oil

Parsley

Cut the peppers in half lengthwise, and remove the seeds. Place on a grilling tray, and put under a hot grill until the skins turn black. Remove from the grill, then place in a plastic food bag. Seal it and leave for 10 minutes to assist in separating the skin from the flesh.

Blend the balsamic vinegar and olive oil in a blender. Season with salt and pepper.

Place the fish on an oven tray, brush with butter or olive oil, season and place in a hot oven for 8 minutes, or until firm to the touch.

Remove the peppers from their bag and remove the skins. Cut the peppers into small dice or diamond shapes and mix with the dressing. heat the dressing on the stove until it is just about to boil.

Place a monkfish steak on to each plate, and spoon the dressing over it. Garnish with parsley and half a lemon.

GERRY WAN

'Nearly every night someone will say "Gerry, make my dinner—just do whatever you like," and I do'

When I moved to Scotland to do a management course at Dundee College, I realised that there were no genuine Cantonese restaurants in this country. After completing my studies, I wanted to do something about this. Even though I had no training as a chef, I decided to start my own business and make a break from the Western/Chinese style of cooking which was around at the time. In 1981 I opened up the Loon Fung Restaurant, cooking authentic Cantonese food.

Within one year, the Loon Fung was in Egon Ronay's *Good Food Guide*. Ten years after that The Peking Inn received recognition from the *Independent* newspaper as 'The Best Chinese Restaurant in Scotland'. Once you are established, you have to maintain your reputation, and to ensure our standards remain high I have had chefs specialising in Dim Sum, cooking and roasting flown over from Hong Kong. The best compliment a restaurant can receive is to have a lot of regular customers, which we have, and to be relied on to serve good food. Nearly every night someone will say: "Gerry, make my dinner—just do whatever you like," and I do.

Although I have performed martial art demonstrations to crowds of more than a thousand people and I am always out chatting to my customers, I am still easily embarrassed. So, with a full house one Saturday night and a queue outside the door, I was horrified when a singing telegram appeared and sang to me for my birthday. It was a really awful experience and I will not be grateful if I am sent another one.

Whenever I can, I travel to China to see what is happening there. This is one of the reasons I am always at the forefront of Chinese cuisine in Scotland—because I do my research well, finding new and exciting dishes to try.

My ambition has always been the same—for my name to be associated with good food. Food has always played a special and dominant role in Chinese culture, and no matter how humble or splendid the surroundings and whatever the reason, the Chinese celebrate by eating.

At The Peking Inn we specialise in seafood and we do our best to have an interesting range of fish and shellfish on offer. Most people are fairly adventurous but the old favourites are hard to beat, so the recipes I have chosen are some of those.

HOT AND SOUR SOUP

100g shredded lean pork or chicken

50g shredded bamboo shoots

2 shredded Chinese mushrooms

50g shrimps

1 block of bean curd (Tofu), cut in fine strips

1 egg

Hot and sour mixture

For the Soup stock:

1 tsp salt

2 tsp soya sauce

4 tsp vinegar

1 tsp chilli oil

3 tsp cornflour

6 tsp water

Mix the stock ingredients all together and bring to the boil in a wok. Add the pork or chicken, shrimps, bamboo shoots and bean curd.

Meanwhile place the dried Chinese mushrooms in cold water for 15 minutes and then cook for 3 minutes with the soup stock.

Add the hot and sour mixture which will thicken the soup.

Finally, beat the egg and pour over the soup. It is now ready to serve.

DRUNKEN CHICKEN

2 chicken breasts

120ml whisky

240ml dry sherry

1 shredded cucumber

50g shredded root ginger

2 bunches of spring onions

Place the chicken breasts, 40g of the root ginger and the spring onions in a cooking wok, add salt, boil and simmer until cooked.

Allow the chicken to cool and then shred.

Pour the whisky and dry sherry over the chicken, completely covering the chicken meat. Soak the chicken for at least 2 hours, preferably leaving it in the fridge overnight.

After the chicken has been marinated, drain the liquid away.

To serve, shred the cucumber and remaining root ginger, and place the chicken on top.

SZECHWAN CRYSTAL KING PRAWN

300g king prawn

1 tsp yellow bean sauce

1 tsp salt

$^1/_2$ tsp cornflour

1 egg white

1 tsp sugar

2 tsp chilli oil

2 tsp vegetable oil

1 fresh chopped chilli

$^1/_4$ green pepper, chopped

$^1/_4$ red pepper, chopped

$^1/_4$ onion, chopped

Remove the prawns from their shells and wash in cold, salted water. Drain well.

Chop the red and green peppers along with the onion.

Heat the vegetable oil in a wok and add the prawns, then stir-fry for 3 minutes. Remove the prawns and drain.

Blend the cornflour with a little water to make a smooth paste.

Combine the salt, egg white, sugar and chilli oil and mix well. Reheat the wok and stir-fry the vegetables and chopped chilli for one minute, then add the salt, egg, sugar and chilli mixture. Add the prawns, and toss and stir for one more minute.

Finally, add the yellow bean sauce and pour in the blended cornflour. Plate and serve.

TOFFEE APPLES

2 apples

2 tsp sesame seeds

For the batter:

100g plain flour

120ml water

1 egg

For the sugar coating:

200g sugar

2 tsp vegetable oil

Heat the oil in a deep-fat fryer.

Segment the apples, removing the core and skin.

Sieve the flour, and add the water and egg. Mix well to form a smooth batter.

Heat 2 teaspoons of vegetable oil in a wok and add the sugar until it has caramelised.
Keep warm.

Dip the apple pieces in the batter and fry until they are golden on the outside.

Apply the hot sugar coating to the apple pieces and then dip them in the sesame
seeds.

Plunge into ice cold water to set the sugar, and set aside to cool. They are now ready
to serve.

GLASGOW ON A PLATE CONTRIBUTORS

AMBER REGENT
50 WEST REGENT STREET
GLASGOW G2
0141 331 1655

BOUZY ROUGE
111 WEST REGENT STREET
GLASGOW G2
0141 221 8804

CAFE GANDOLFI
64 ALBION STREET
GLASGOW G1
0141 552 6813

CITY MERCHANT
97 CANDLERIGGS
GLASGOW G1
0141 553 1577

THE COOK'S ROOM
205 FENWICK ROAD
GIFFNOCK
GLASGOW G46
0141 621 1903

EURASIA
150 ST VINCENT STREET
GLASGOW G2
0141 204 1150

GAMBA
225A WEST GEORGE STREET
GLASGOW G2
0141 572 0899

THE INN ON THE GREEN
25 GREENHEAD STREET
GLASGOW G40
0141 554 0165

LA PARMIGIANA
447 GREAT WESTERN ROAD
GLASGOW G12
0141 334 0686

THE MARINER AT THE MOAT HOUSE
CONGRESS ROAD
GLASGOW G3
0141 306 9988

MITCHELLS
157 NORTH STREET
GLASGOW G3
0141 204 4312

NAIRN'S
13 WOODSIDE CRESCENT
GLASGOW G3
0141 353 0707

ONE DEVONSHIRE GARDENS
1 DEVONSHIRE GARDENS
GLASGOW G12
0141 339 2001

PEKING INN
191 HOPE STREET
GLASGOW G2
0141 332 7120

ROGANO
11 EXCHANGE PLACE
GLASGOW G1
0141 248 4055

STRAVAIGIN
28 GIBSON STREET
GLASGOW G12
0141 334 2665

UBIQUITOUS CHIP
12 ASHTON LANE
GLASGOW G12
0141 334 5007

YES
22 WEST NILE STREET
GLASGOW G1
0141 221 8623

LIST OF RECIPES